The SIXTH MAN

The SIXTH MAN

A SEASON INSIDE the NBA PLAYGROUND

CHRIS PALMER

ESPN BOOKS

**ESPN
BOOKS**
a division of
ESPN publishing

CONTENTS

INTRODUCTION

AS WE PULLED UP to the decrepit street corner in South Central Los Angeles two years ago, Clippers guard Andre Miller used the driver's side controls to roll down the passenger's side window—my window. That's when I noticed the guy making his way to the car. He had to be one of L.A.'s original gangstas.

He wore a wife beater and house slippers and had an unlit cigarette dangling from his ashy lips. His eyes were bloodshot red. On his knuckles, he had tattooed the words DIE TRYIN. Dude looked at me like I was a bitch.

I thought about my hotel room in sunny Santa Monica, the one with the spectacular view of the ocean. I pictured the headline in tomorrow's paper: NBA STAR AND SOME REPORTER JACKED ON CRENSHAW. How was I going to explain new underwear on my expense report?

"Wassup, Killer? How's your family?" Andre said to the man.

"We cool. It's on and crackin', you know how Killer's peeps do," he replied.

"This is my man from ESPN," said Andre, pointing to me. "He's out here doing a story on me."

A grin spread across Killer's face, revealing two gold fronts. He extended the hand with R-Y-I-N and gave me a firm shake. His eyes shifted as we talked. He kept looking over the rooftop of the car as if he was expecting 5–0 or worse to roll around the corner.

"ESPN, huh?" he said. "That sounds like a cool job. I bet you get to meet all kinds of people, see all kinds of stuff. You ever seen a place like this?"

Now, I've chased stories in the crumbling rowhouses of North Philly and the cold concrete projects of Coney Island, but South Central's precarious history is glorified in music, television, and rap videos. I can't lie. I was a little scared as Andre guided his mom's Honda (he feared his BMW 735i would attract too much attention) through neighborhoods the L.A. police were too scared to patrol. I knew Miller's basketball rep would buy us some protection, but it wasn't going to stop a stray bullet.

What can I say? My writer's imagination was brimming with adrenaline.

Turns out Andre used to play Pop Warner football with this guy Killer. While the former was gearing up to run the point for L.A., the latter was trying to put his life together after a three-year bid for possession. For the next two hours, Andre and I drove around South Central visiting his mom's house, his old barbershop, and the other landmarks of his childhood. My tape recorder hummed as he talked about his roots. I sat quietly, watching the check-cashing joints and liquor stores sail by. *Damn, this is real*, I thought, *not some NWA video*. I didn't have to take Tupac's word anymore.

Four hours later, I found myself in Beverly Hills. After a couple of frantic calls from a cell phone with lousy reception, Shaquille O'Neal's publicist steered me in the direction of his client's estate. I climbed the winding street lined with ten-foot-tall, neatly manicured bushes, marveling at the bling. I half expected to find a sign that said ANYTHING WITH LESS THAN 24-INCH RIMS WILL

BE TOWED. I parked my Oldsmobile rental behind an Aston Martin and made my way to the door.

Do I ring the bell or just enter? The polite thing to do was announce my arrival. But then I ran the risk of standing on the doorstep like a jerk because no one could hear the damn thing over the stereo. My high school coach always told me to "fake it 'til you can make it." (Usually when I was on the bench watching other people fake it).

So, what the hell? I strolled in like I owned the place. Pulled open the front door and, much to my relief, heard no alarms or barking dobermans. I was dazzled by the grandness of the foyer. High ceilings, marble floors, beautiful paintings. A six-foot statue of a knight with a removable sword that would have been mine if only I could have fit it in the Oldsmobile's trunk. In a matter of hours, I'd climbed from one of the poorest zip codes in America to one of the richest. Talk about movin' on up. Even George Jefferson called to give me props.

I pressed on to the back of the house, passing two rather attractive pieces of arm candy. They smiled. *I must belong*, I thought. I came to a wide-open room with black leather couches and a seventy-two-inch, plasma flat-screen TV, complete with Playstation 2 and, like, five DVD players. I could picture the realtor telling Shaq how much flow the room had. Great for entertaining. Lots of sunlight.

A guy who looked like Jeremy Piven was sitting on the couch playing Vice City solo. I went ahead and assumed it was Jeremy Piven. "Great job on that last thing you did," I said in a pathetic attempt to speak Hollywood.

"Thanks, man. I got roasted for that shit," he replied. "You wanna play?"

"Cool. I'll get us some drinks."

I hustled to the back patio, where I discovered a small crowd of people who looked rich, bored and/or self-important, drinking martinis and eating olives as Coldplay eased from the speakers. No Shaq. Not even his bodyguard. *Jerome, where you at?* I grabbed two Coronas, hustled back to the game room, and handed one to "Jeremy." He had the game cued up.

He took Player 1. He clearly had skills. Still, I knew I could crush him without trying. I had decided ahead of time to let him win, though. People hate losing to strangers. Besides, it would give us something to talk about when I saw him later at the party.

"Remember that time I smoked you in Vice City," he'd say, showing off for the arm candy. And I'd go, "Yeah, great times, man!"

Well, about seven minutes into the game, his cell phone started up. The ring tone was set to the G Unit's "Stunt 101." *Nice.*

"I've gotta take this, bro," he said, excusing himself. "Be right back." He paused the game and I knocked back the rest of my Corona. I don't even like beer. After five minutes, I started to get restless. After fifteen, I unpaused the game and killed his man. After thirty-five, I got up to mingle with the *Maxim* model-like girls sipping fruity drinks. I wasn't really famous so they weren't really talking. I grabbed another Corona, sat back on the couch, and searched in vain for someone I knew. *Man, I wish Killer was here.*

After about forty-five minutes, "Jeremy" finally returned, unaware that I had jacked his man. I was psyched to see a familiar face.

"My bad, bro," he said. "You know how it is."

Do I ever.

"No prob," I replied. "But, man, don't you think it's pretty lame that Shaq didn't even show up at his own thing?"

"What thing?"

"This thing. Shaq, man. He throws a get together and he doesn't even come."

"Dude, this isn't Shaq's house."

Game over.

THERE'S A CERTAIN CALM that fills a locker room before an NBA game. The empty stools. Unattended lockers. Crisp, unworn shoes without creases. I like to zero in on one of the jerseys hanging on the hooks and think to myself, *someone in Duluth is going to see that uniform on* SportsCenter *tonight.* When I read the name on the back, I start to wonder what forces conspired to bring that individual together with these eleven others at this moment in time? Deng. Duhon. Hinrich. Gordon. Nocioni. Chandler. Curry. Think about it. Five years ago, these guys didn't know each other. They were scattered across the globe. And yet, despite astronomical odds, they all ended up in Chicago, on the same Bulls team, living, traveling, winning, losing, laughing, and crying side by side. The only thing more remarkable in my mind is that I myself am in their midst, earning a paycheck to chronicle their stories.

Don't get me wrong. Like every boy who owned a basketball in America, I once dreamed of playing in the league—of making that leap from South Central to Beverly Hills on draft night. But somehow the forces that guided my life forgot to load me up with the prerequisite skills. And so, today I find myself pursuing a slightly different career path.

How did I get here? Well, you might say it started with a murder.

I killed Brad Davis. I really did. The University of Maryland guard never saw it coming. I was sitting on the shag carpet in my parents' sunken living room, inches from their brand new twenty-one-inch color RCA, watching the University of Maryland and North Carolina State duke it out in the Atlantic Coast Conference Tournament. This was the late Seventies and I wasn't much of a fan, being a toddler and all. Sure, I'd heard my mother, a certified hoop fanatic, speak of her fondness for Davis, the wild-haired Terrapins star with the short shorts that left little to the imagination. But the game's allure was lost on me, what with Lincoln Logs and the precious few of my Hot Wheels collection that hadn't become wedged in the creepy darkness beneath the living room couch.

I'm not sure what made me do it. Perhaps it was a Stewie Griffinesque plan to rid the world of the competition—anyone who vied with me for my mother's attention. All I know is that, when the opportunity presented itself, I crawled to the occasion.

Davis was standing with his parted hair and bad cop mustache at the free-throw line. As he let out a slow breath and raised the ball above his head, taking aim at the glossy red ring in front of him, I reached up to the screen and placed his scrawny body between my index finger and thumb, squishing him like a bug.

"You just killed Brad Davis," my mother shrieked, sending her knitting needles flying.

She must have forgiven me. Because on my sixth birthday, she gave me a red-and-white basketball with the word COLLEGIATE stamped on it. I don't remember any of the other type, but I'm sure OFFICIAL and INFLATE were on there, too. Now I vaguely recall hearing the word *collegiate* in the fuzzy moments before the Davis incident and I couldn't very well have something like that linking me to my crime. So every day after school, I proceeded to the court on the gentle, downhill slope behind Magnolia Elementary, not fifteen minutes by car from the University of Maryland campus. The asphalt had recently been outlined in a thick orange-yellow paint that broke away in chips the size of bologna slices when you kicked at it. Hour after hour, I bounced that red-and-white sphere off the onyx asphalt, marveling at the ping sound it made every time it connected with the ground, while laboring to erase the evidence from my ball.

Triumphantly, I watched that pebble grain begin to yield. The ball's surface gradually got smoother. COLLEGIATE began to fade, erased bit by bit from all knowledge. By week's end, the offending word was gone. But then something happened that I didn't expect. I started enjoying what I was doing. I was hooked. I could handle the ball without looking at it. Dribble it high above my waist or inches from the ground. I could zip it between my legs, run at full speed without losing control and, with a little practice, send it zooming behind my back. In the space of three weeks, I went from awkwardly launching it with two hands, usually over the backboard, to making five out of ten shots with proper form from the number two on the hopscotch grid.

I watched what the older kids did and tried to apply what I saw when no one was around. I screened games on TV and tried to memorize moves. When my parents bought a Sony Betamax, I taped games and viewed them over and over again. Since I had no means to purchase videotapes, I simply recorded over what was available— usually my mom's and dad's *Dallas* episodes and the occasional home movie.

I quickly became an astute observer of every team in the area. The Washington Bullets with their earthbound power forward Wes Unseld. Maryland's Terps and their wonderful backcourt of Len Bias and Keith Gatlin. The awesome juggernaut that was Patrick Ewing and the Georgetown Hoyas. For a subsequent birthday, along with the first Garfield book by Jim Davis, my parents bought me a dark blue and gray Hoyas jersey. I loved that gift and wore it nearly everywhere (including to bed). Even after I discovered that my V-neck collar was slightly different than the one Ewing wore on TV. Unwittingly, I was modeling my first throwback.

I did everything in my power to soak up every last morsel of basketball. Between *Sports Illustrated* and ESPN broadcasts, I flirted with stimulation overload. In the summer months, I'd climb from bed while my parents were still sleeping to relieve my dad's *Washington Post* of the sports section. The pages would still be warm, literally hot off the presses. I'd scan the eight-point type in the transactions blurbs, looking for news about contracts, trades, and recruiting. As I graduated to junior high, I began counting the days until the preview guides hit the newsstands. I loved reading about the lives of my favorite players. A photo of the basketball court in Larry Bird's front yard in French Lick, Indiana, is forever etched in my mind. An article on hotshot high school senior Kenny Anderson from Queens sparked an interest in the playgrounds of New York. In the *Washington Post*, I read that University of Maryland star Len Bias improved his ballhandling by dribbling in a darkened room. So I went down to the basement, flipped off the switch, and worked on becoming Georgetown's next blue-chip recruit. By the time I turned the lights back on, I'd surrendered my allowance for a year. Sadly, nothing can replace those handmade Christmas decorations.

My parents gave me Charles Dickens and John Steinbeck for Christmas, but I quickly put them down when I couldn't find anything in their pages on the pick-and-roll. When my mother brought home from the library a copy of John Feinstein's *A Season on the Brink*, though, I read it three times. She was a sport and covered the late fees. Next I devoured Mitch Albom's *Fab Five*, Sam Smith's *The*

Jordan Rules, and everything written by Nelson George. I'd hide away in my room reading and re-reading the *Big East College Basketball Yearbook,* a regional preview that almost always featured my favorite Hoya on the cover. After that, I'd tackle the *ACC Yearbook.* I wondered if people on the West Coast were flipping through a Pac-10 edition.

In the summer of 1987, I wrote to the sports information departments at Georgetown and UNLV requesting team media guides. Neither responded. I was not dismayed, because I soon discovered a piece of literature that changed my life. On a muggy August day, I walked into a tinderbox of a high school gym in Prince George's County to watch an Amateur Athletic Union game. As I climbed the rickety bleachers, a small, dog-eared magazine not much bigger than a *TV Guide* caught my eye. The mustard-colored pages were covered with blue type. A crude logo read HOOP SCOOP. The Os were little red basketballs. Published by a man named Clark Francis, the magazine was less a journalistic masterpiece than a nuts-and-bolts scouting report. What I read captivated me.

Writing from his home in Louisville, Kentucky, Francis did not spare the reader his opinion. There was a story on the invitation-only Nike Camp, complete with evaluations on each of the 120 players in attendance. About Mike Hopkins, a 6-foot-4 guard from Santa Ana, California, he wrote, "high school coach works camp— wouldn't be here otherwise." He praised 6-foot-9 Robert Horry as "the best passing big forward in camp...powers inside with authority and is fundamentally sound." Sam Cassell, a senior point guard from Baltimore, was an "outstanding floor general...excellent passer...always in control." That was the first time I'd heard the term floor general. From that day forward, it was part of my lexicon. (Although *lexicon* wasn't part of my lexicon until years later.) Jimmy Jackson of Toledo, Ohio, was "great in transition...a gusto dunker...comparable to Magic Johnson...smooth as cashmere." From Riverdale, Maryland, came Henry Hall, "a little point guard who loves to shoot." I made a note of that. Hall started for the local AAU powerhouse that day and hit eight threes. He went on to lead the D.C. Metro area in scoring with 37 points a game.

My own career would play itself out in that gym over the next few years with a mix of triumph and anguish. But that day I became a true student of the game. Articulating what I'd learned became as important to me as actually playing the game. I developed a keen interest in the written word.

My mother wrote regularly for a local newspaper called *The Prince George's Journal* and occasionally for *The Post*. She mostly covered the country music scene. I'd tag along to Wolf Trap and Merriweather Post Pavilion, sitting at her side, quietly swinging my feet back and forth, as she interviewed stars like Willie Nelson, Ricky Skaggs, and Gordon Lightfoot. The day after a concert, I'd sit outside the door to her workroom, listening as she banged out her stories on a red IBM Selectric typewriter. Each tap on the keys sounded like an exploding firecracker. We'd drive to the grocery store in our 1972 Dodge Coronet and buy copies of the paper. It was a thrill to see my mom's name in print. I loved reading the stories and thinking, *I was there for that.*

My mother's journalism career inevitably gave way to shuttling me back and forth to basketball practice and games, and occasionally to rebounding for me on the courts at Magnolia, but I never forgot the thrill of being on the inside. When my ballhandling skills betrayed me, I simply picked up a notebook and a pen. It was my way of staying in the game. In the fall of my freshman year at Howard University, *Washington Post* columnist Michael Wilbon came to speak to a select group of students in the school's journalism program. He took a seat at a round table in front of the classroom, my professor to his right and me to his left. I had taken several days to prepare my questions. I wanted to challenge Wilbon, to show him I was his equal. But when it came time to speak, curiosity got the better of me.

"Why are you here with us?" I asked. "Shouldn't you be over at Georgetown watching the next big thing in basketball?"

The Hoyas' 1994–95 season opened that night with an exhibition game against Fort Hood.

"I've seen so many next big things who never amounted to anything," Wilbon said, a touch annoyed. "What makes you think this one is going to be any different?"

"I've got a feeling," I replied rather weakly.

So much for the intelligent back and forth.

I was right, though. Allen Iverson would go on to become one of the greatest players of all time.

Wilbon was then one of just six African-American sports columnists working at a major newspaper. Before *The Post* offered him a column, he had fielded offers from *Sports Illustrated*. "I could have taken a cushy magazine job for six figures and been content," he said. But he wanted to make certain his voice would be heard. He was helping to blaze a trail.

He went on to talk candidly about the rewards, financial and personal, of rising to the upper echelon of the journalism world. The Mitsubishi Diamante parked out by the curb was proof enough for me. As Wilbon drove off into the night, I sat on a weather-beaten bench deep in thought. One of my idols had just given me an hour of his time, dispensing pearls of wisdom from his many years in the business. Suddenly, my career path was crystal clear. I wanted a cushy magazine job.

Three years later, as an intern at *USA Today*, I found myself face to face with Iverson I walked into the locker room at the MCI Center and saw him signing glossy basketball cards with a black Sharpie. "My mother does this bullshit every game," he said. (Ann Iverson has this habit of promising her son's autograph to all her friends.) I nervously walked up to him and extended my tape recorder.

"I want to ask you about ..." I said.

Iverson looked at me as if I had just insulted the very woman he was cursing.

"Nah, man," he said in that gravely voice of his. "I don't talk before games."

"Uh, OK, I'll catch you afterwards," I replied, backing away with my tail between my legs.

Lesson Number One: Not all NBA players talk before the game.

Kobe Bryant did talk. I stood six inches from the first-time All-Star that same season as he addressed a dozen high-profile media types in front of his locker. I dominated that question-and-answer session. It was a bold move for a college intern, but I wasn't the least bit intimidated. Kobe had a piece of spinach stuck between his teeth.

As I left the locker room, a reporter I know was asking Shaq about the craziest thing a female fan had ever done to win him over. Shaq had a whole list of answers. "We were in Milwaukee," he said, flashing that giant smile at me, "and this girl—I'm telling you she was a ten, no *eleven*—came to the door of my hotel room wearing a trench coat."

He paused for effect, putting his arm around me.

"Nothing but a trench coat." He laughed. "I'm telling you, bro, it was a set up."

OVER THE COURSE OF five seasons on the NBA beat for *ESPN The Magazine*, I've worked my way into many circles and become the trusted voice of a young generation of millionaire athletes. Not yet ten years removed from the same high school camps that shaped them, I walk the walk and talk the talk. I first met Darius Miles at the Staples Center in December of 2000, when his NBA career was less than a month old. Within minutes, we were singing or, more precisely, butchering the chorus of Outkast's "Ms. Jackson." In April of 2001, *The Magazine* sent me to cover a first-round playoff series between the Bucks and the Magic. Over dinner one night, I found myself commiserating with Rafer Alston and Michael over the fact that George Karl, their coach, was less committed to their futures than those of Sam Cassell and Ray Allen. In June of that year, I found myself at a photo shoot in Long Beach, California, tossing a Nerf football on the sand with Bulls draft picks Eddy Curry and Tyson Chandler. The two were amused when I bragged about my arm. The stocky Curry tossed lithe, 7-foot-1 Chandler a little ten-yard strike. As Chandler jogged toward me in his bare feet, I lowered my shoulder and hit him square in the midsection. I lifted the future of the Bulls on my back and pumped my fist. We all had a laugh and tossed the Nerf until the photography assistants brought lunch.

"How come you're not in any of the pictures?" one of them asked.

"Because I don't play for the Bulls," I said.

Though it sounds absurd, I've been the beneficiary of that mistaken impression before—often enough to wonder how simple it would be to leave my ordinary life behind. To bravely go where the TV cameras cannot. Deep inside a world where 19-year-old high school grads earn $20 million dollars a year, where Jay-Z regularly pops up on your caller I.D., where the finest clothes, the fastest cars, and the sweetest women are the perks of the job. All I'd have to do was convince five of the game's hottest young players to open their lives to me, I told my boss, and I could write the definitive book on the NBA life, a funny, insightful *Almost Famous* look at the highs and lows of professional basketball. Like Visa, I'd be everywhere you want to be. In the homes, the cars, the hotel rooms, the parties, the nightclubs and the dinner conversations of genuine players. Guys with compelling stories and plenty at stake in the months ahead. Simple, right? I scribbled the names of potential candidates on a piece of paper: Jamal Crawford of the Knicks, Tracy McGrady of the Rockets, Carmelo Anthony of the Nuggets, Dwight Howard of the Magic, Baron Davis of the Hornets and Elton Brand of the Clippers. I had a great rapport with those guys. They all respected my work.

On opening night of the 2004–05 season, I sat at my desk in *ESPN The Magazine's* midtown Manhattan offices amidst a clutter of media guides, pouring over schedules and planning my route. *Let's see. If I spend three days in Miami for games with the Sonics and the Knicks, jump a jet to Los Angeles to catch a Lakers game against the Rockets and a Clippers game against the Suns, I can stop off in Detroit for two games, two shoot-arounds and a practice on my way back to New York. That leaves me with a day and a half to stock up on clean underwear before I hit the road again. Keep up the pace for eight more months and everything will be fine. Just remind me to pick out a tombstone for my social life.*

Have you ever read the children's story about the clever little monkey who convinces a lion that he's the most fearsome animal in the jungle? "I can prove it to you," the monkey says. "Just walk behind me as I make my way through the jungle." The lion agrees. Every animal they pass—a giraffe, a hippo, a gorilla—flees with a shriek. "I say," says the lion, "you are the most feared creature in the jungle."

Well, that's me, the monkey. Come meet the lions.

GAME ON

NEW YORK CITY, NOVEMBER 6, 2004

IT'S AN HOUR BEFORE tip-off. In the front row, two seats to the left of Spike Lee, sits Jamal Crawford. After four years in basketball purgatory with the Chicago Bulls, the 24-year-old shooting guard has landed himself a $56 million contract to play in Madison Square Garden—the greatest stage in basketball. Not thirty minutes earlier, in a tunnel beside the court, Isiah Thomas—another recent New York Knicks acquisition—was telling MSG analyst and former Knick great Walt "Clyde" Frazier how badly he wants to win this first home opener as the team's president.

The Knicks lure more business suits than any other team in the NBA. At times, it looks as if half the fans in the Garden's lower seats are outfitted by Brooks Brothers. Problem is folks like those don't make a lot of noise. They're there on some my-boss-is-out-of-town-so-he-gave-me-the-company-tickets sort of deal. But maybe, just maybe, if a player with a wicked crossover and an unbridled open-court game were to sport the orange and blue, those fans would put down their $9 beers and cheer. That's what Thomas is thinking. "Damn, I want to win this one tonight," he says, his eyes lighting up. "This is everything."

The public address announcer introduces Crawford and hands him a microphone. The player walks to center court to deliver a message to 20,000 people giddy with the promise of a fresh start. "I just want to tell you how much I appreciate the way you all have embraced me," Crawford says. "This is going to be a great season for us. We're going to have some good times and some bad times, but I'm here to let you know that we're taking it straight to the playoffs."

A great roar goes up from the crowd.

Although the Knicks have one of the league's highest payrolls, some $40 million over the NBA's salary cap, they have precious little to show for it. Thomas's predecessor, Scott Layden, put a halt to the city's great postseason clashes with Michael Jordan's Bulls and Reggie Miller's Pacers in his five years at the helm, stocking the roster with marginal athletes who all seemed to play power forward. During his tenure, the team's record was a disheartening 204–206 with one trip to the conference finals, one first-round playoff exit, and three postseasons on the couch.

So there's hope in the building on this night, but plenty of skepticism, too. Seconds into the game, the new-look Knicks look lethargic. The Celtics—coached by former Knick Doc Rivers—beat them to every loose ball. Paul Pierce is a one-man wrecking crew, playing as if his life depends on the outcome. Crawford, on the other hand, can't seem to find his rhythm. He misses his first shot, a fifteen-footer from the right baseline, banging it off the side of the rim and pressing onward for nine points, two assists, and 2-of-5 shooting from the field in the first half.

For much of the second half, boos rain down from the rafters. New York trails by 31 to start the fourth. I keep waiting for Isiah to halt play and send Crawford back to center court with his microphone. "No, seriously, we're just messin' with you guys," he'd say. "We're gonna start playing for real now." Ashton Kutcher would pop up behind the Knicks' bench to tell us we'd all been punk'd. What a gag it would be. Sadly, that never happens. The 107–73 debacle is the worst home-opening loss in the Knicks' fifty-nine year history.

Sandwiched in a gloomy corner of the room between the lockers of Allan Houston and Stephon Marbury, Crawford tries to sum up his feelings. He fled Chicago to escape nights like this. "I don't know what to tell you guys," he says, easing himself into a navy blue suit. "I didn't expect this. I didn't expect us to come out like this. I'm just stunned."

He knots his tie and slips his bare feet into size fifteen dress shoes. "I don't blame the fans for booing as hard as they did," he says, "because we deserved it. Man, not even in Chicago did we get booed that hard. If I was them, I'd have booed, too."

NEW ORLEANS, NOVEMBER 9

HERE'S A BIT OF wisdom I've picked up on the beat. If you want to avoid conversations with perfect strangers, don't mention two things: 1) that you call New York City home and 2) that you cover basketball for a living. I do both shortly after catching a cab outside my hotel in the French Quarter. Lucky for me, the silver-haired cabbie, Julius, is cool.

"Why the Knicks ain't try and get Shaq?" he asks. "They didn't have the money?"

"They were strapped," I reply. "Not even in the running."

"Well, I'll tell you who is playing good right now. What's that white boy from Russia name?"

"You mean Dirk Nowitzki? I think he's from Germany."

"Yeah, that's him. He's just killin' folk. You know he's like a white Larry Bird."

"True, true."

"Ain't have no money for Shaq, huh? You know I don't like Isiah Thomas. Not after he did Adrian Dantley that way. He brought in his boy to replace him. Mark McGwire. That wasn't right. Nobody couldn't stop Dantley one-on-one. Nobody. Certainly not Mark McGwire."

I'm with you all the way, J, though I think you mean Mark *Aguirre*.

Outside the arena, I slip the cabbie a little something extra and fight through the crowd to the media entrance, only to watch the Hornets fall 31 points behind the Lakers then make a furious-but-futile run to a 106–98 loss. "It's very easy to come back and lose," says Hornets head coach Byron Scott.

Afterwards, I make a beeline for Baron Davis's locker to invite the Hornets' All-Star point guard to join my project. Along the way, I stop to chat up New Orleans' free-spirited forward, Chris Andersen, who's wearing a mink coat and ambling toward the players' family lounge to meet his Barbie-looking girlfriend. He wraps me in a bear hug.

"Whassup, pimp?" he says, "Everything cool with you?"

"How's your nose, dude?" I ask. He took a vicious elbow in the second quarter.

"Aw fuck, man, I had to breathe out of my mouth the whole game. Almost broke my shit."

"Chris Mihm did that shit, in case you didn't know," I tell him.

"No shit."

"Yeah, but I'll catch up with you. I gotta go find B.D."

"Aiight, pimp, hit me up."

"Cool."

The lockerroom is empty save for Davis.

"Tough one tonight, huh man?" is all I can think to say.

Davis shakes his head and cracks a smile. "Who you telling? Man, we need a win. This is bullshit."

I give him a handshake followed by a half hug. I haven't seen him since last season. In the midst of catching up, I realize that he's naked. I look away and try to project my voice. Davis keeps right on talking. This is an NBA locker room, after all. But how am I supposed to ask him to expose himself to heightened scrutiny under these circumstances? Getting him to agree to cooperate will be a long shot after a loss like this. Better to catch him when he's fully clothed. By then—hopefully—the Hornets' fortunes will have improved.

"Man, we need a win bad," says Davis.

Yeah, really. And for God's sake, young man, put some clothes on.

ORLANDO, NOVEMBER 12

I'M THINKING THAT A fish-out-of-water rookie storyline might be a good idea. Say, for example, a wide-eyed, 18-year-old, devout Christian trying to make his way in the hip-hopified NBA. And sure enough, late in the third quarter of his sixth professional game, Dwight Howard's eyes are as big as saucers.

Kobe Bryant has just shaken his man, leaving Howard all alone to defend the basket. The rookie thinks he can challenge Bryant's shot. He thinks wrong. Howard takes a half-step forward and Bryant lifts off quicker than expected. Before Howard can cover his head, Bryant—eye level with the rim—throws a monster dunk down his throat, sending both benches into a frenzy.

Duh-duh-duh, duh-duh-duh.

A chorus of giggly, grown men chanting the *SportsCenter* theme confronts Howard in the post-game shower, sending peals of laughter rising up with the steam. One by one, the Orlando players return to their lockers, fighting to conceal their snickers. When Howard emerges from the suds, the injured Cuttino Mobley is lying in wait.

"Young fella," he says. "You're now officially in the league."

Steve Francis intervenes to rescue the rookie's fragile ego. "Everybody gets dunked on by Kobe Bryant," he explains. "I've been dunked on by Kobe plenty of times. All that means is you're one of us now." Howard lowers his head and smiles, revealing a mouthful of braces. Minutes later, he leaves the locker room looking like a new man, but not before one last parting shot from his teammates. "Watch your head boy!"

Howard smiles sheepishly when I stop him in the hallway. "Hey, man, don't worry about that dunk," I say playfully. "It happens to the best of us." Before I can steer the conversation to my bright idea for an all-access book, a second wave of laughter interrupts us. Howard's Atlanta high school pals are rumbling down the hallway, howling with delight.

I pry Howard's cousin, Kevin Samples, now his manager, away long enough to run the notion by him. He tells me to call Dwight's agent, Aaron Goodwin. Not exactly the "Great idea, man!" I was looking for. This is turning out to be a lot harder than I anticipated.

HOUSTON, NOVEMBER 18

IN THE SPRING OF 1999, I met Tracy McGrady in the lobby of a Holiday Inn in Secaucus, New Jersey. I'd just received my first assignment as a cub reporter for *The Magazine*, a small story on two young cousins who played for the Toronto Raptors. Vince Carter sat on my left, Tracy

McGrady on my right. Carter was chatty. McGrady wanted to go upstairs and finish his pregame nap. I was so nervous I forgot to turn on the tape recorder.

In September of 2001, I met him for the second time outside the Casa Del Mar hotel in Santa Monica. The sun was in my eyes. I didn't see him until he was right up on me. "Aw, man, I know this dude," he said, stepping onto the curb. "What's up? What do you got there?"

He eyed the stack of CDs in my hand.

"You get that new Jay-Z yet?" he asked.

"Nah. Not yet."

"What? What's wrong with this dude?" he said to no one in particular.

"I heard it was tight? Is it on the level of *Reasonable Doubt*?"

"Way better. Better then *Vol. 2*"

"Better than *Vol. 2*? Damn!"

"It's been out damn near a week and you still don't have it? I'll bring it tonight."

We traveled by limo to a commercial shoot for his Adidas sneaker, the T-Mac 1. In a trailer on the set, we ate Domino's Pizza and listened to Jay-Z's *The Blueprint*. McGrady knew almost every word. That interview was markedly different. Tracy talked a lot of shit. He was loose and confident. He loves to speak off the record about players' games.

In the wee hours of the morning, McGrady, his crew-cut, muscle-bound trainer, and I retreated to a penthouse suite in the Casa Del Mar to chow down some takeout and watch *Three Kings*. Halfway through the movie, Wayne Hall, the trainer, said goodnight. McGrady pleaded with him to hang just a little while longer. He's always hated to be alone.

Before tonight's showdown with the Knicks, I find him wide awake—and alone—in the Rockets' locker room at the Toyota Center in downtown Houston.

"You ready, man?"

"I'm always ready," McGrady replies.

I fully expect this response. As a shellshocked rookie in Toronto in 1997, fresh off a leap from the relative warmth of Mount Zion Christian Academy in Durham, North Carolina, to the cold, hard facts of his new life in Canada, McGrady did what any troubled 18-year-old would do: He slept—sometimes for up to twenty hours in a day. His coach, Darrell Walker, not only viewed this as unacceptable, he labeled McGrady a slacker in the press. McGrady quickly dispelled that myth, working hard to become the league's leading scorer in Orlando. But his rep took another major blow when the Magic lost sixty-one games last season. In a very public spat, Orlando's first-year general manager questioned McGrady's commitment to the team. So Houston represents a fresh start, a golden opportunity to silence his critics while playing beside the mighty Yao Ming. But nothing short of a world championship will suffice.

On the court, the 4–5 Rockets have a long way to go. After the Knicks slice them up for 32 fourth-quarter points, McGrady finds himself with the ball at the top of the key, trying to protect a two-point lead. With the game clock winding down, he explodes to the basket, missing a runner from eight feet out. The Knicks grab the rebound and call time with 2.9 seconds to go.

New York coach Lenny Wilkens draws up an inbounds play designed to give Jamal Crawford a three-point shot from the right wing. Crawford has connected on 4-of-10 attempts from beyond the arc in the game's first forty-seven minutes. "Don't worry, I'm going to make this," he says to his teammates.

Anfernee Hardaway's inbounds pass is off the mark. Crawford has to run to catch it. He takes two quick dribbles toward the three-point line and chucks up an off-balance prayer that drills the backboard and swishes through the hoop. He high steps down the floor like a maniac.

McGrady lowers his head and somberly walks off the court.

HOBOKEN, NEW JERSEY, NOVEMBER 19

MY TIMING IS IMPECCABLE. I arrive home from the office just in time to catch *SportsCenter* and, to my surprise, I find that they've recast the top of the show. No upbeat music. No anchors hyping highlights. The tone is decidedly somber—almost as if someone's died. Moving around my living room in a hurry-up offense, turning on lights and sorting the mail, I hear the words "worst brawl in American sports history." I stop cold and settle onto the couch with my jacket half off.

Earlier this evening, ESPN broadcast the Pacers-Pistons game. Instead of showing clips of the action, *SportsCenter* replays the final minute of play as if cutting to a live game. The Pacers are up 97–82. Ben Wallace drives the lane for a garbage hoop. Before he can complete the play, he's fouled hard by Indiana's Ron Artest. Wallace gives Artest a shove, then charges him. Both players have to be restrained.

As the refs huddle to iron things out, Artest reclines on the scorer's table. A cup of ice rains down on him from the stands. In an instant, the volatile Pacer forward leaps the table and charges the wrong fan. Stephen Jackson runs to his teammate's aid swinging wildly at everyone in sight. Madness overtakes The Palace. With an overhand right, Artest drops a fan on the court wearing a Pistons jersey. Jermaine O'Neal steps in to defend Artest. The melee escalates into a full-scale riot between players and fans. "Oh, this is a disgrace," a dejected Bill Walton repeats over and over on the air.

As a fan of the sport, I too am horrified. My stomach sinks when I think of the players I know on both teams. Over the next few weeks, their colleagues in the league will speculate on how they would've reacted under the circumstances. Some will support Artest. Others will not. But very few will blame him. "You got to protect yourself at all times," an Eastern Conference guard tells me. "As players, sometimes we take a lot of abuse from fans. It comes with the job, but you have to draw the line when people start throwing things at you. They're messing with your livelihood. But what do you do? Because if you cross that line, there are going to be serious consequences. What did Artest lose? That was a $6 million mistake. Who wants to lose $6 million over a fan?"

NEW YORK, NOVEMBER 21

I MAKE MY WAY down the Garden steps to the courtside seats beside the visitors' bench. Due to the sheer number of reporters who cover the Knicks, I don't often find myself so close to the shiny hardwood. I'm usually assigned to Box 64 about twenty rows up behind the Knicks' bench. Down here, you see the game from a whole different perspective. For starters, I notice the leggy blonde sitting in Celebrity Row. Every couple of minutes, she pulls out a compact and runs her fingers through her bangs. When the Garden's savvy celebrity spotters flash her image on the big screen, the crowd begins to chant "Par-is Hilton! Par-is Hil-ton!"

I should have known, what with her being more consumed with her hair than with LeBron James. I'm not here to knock the heiress, though. I love Paris. I really do. Every so often, I catch her looking in my direction. At first, kind of casual-like. Then more blatantly. Now she's literally staring at me.

I once learned by watching *Oprah* that a member of the opposite sex is interested in you if she stares at you for more than seven seconds. Paris has easily exceeded ten and we're not even out of the first quarter. And, come to think of it, we've been down this road before, at the 2004 All-Star Game in L.A. As Paris walked arm in arm with her then-boyfriend Nick Carter to the private celebrity halftime retreat, she cocked her head ever so slightly and we locked eyes. I was sitting with the press about ten rows up. She held my gaze for about one and a half seconds. She wasn't exactly frowning. Those may be the most useless seconds of her life, but all my friends have heard the story. I know I'm pathetic, but come on, a guy can dream can't he?

But with The Heiress flipping her hair and staring holes in my forehead, I'm moments away from folding under the pressure. I try to steady myself by watching LeBron. When I look up, Ms. Hilton has vacated her seat.

No, no, wait, she's coming back. And, as she sits down, she gives me (and about 5,000 other people) an eyeful. Now I can say I've seen Paris Hilton's underwear. The sideline photographers are going berserk. I peer over the shoulder of a perverted-looking fellow who's spinning the click wheel on his digital camera searching for the money shot.

That's when it hits me: Paris wasn't looking at me. She was posing for the cameras. What a fool I am!

With the Knicks leading Cleveland 51–38 at the half, I vow to put her out of my mind. It's over between us—right after I get a closer look. I generally exit through the players' tunnel but this time I bolt to the celebrities' tunnel on the opposite end of the court. With everyone rushing to the restrooms, though, Paris has managed to give me the slip. I weave through the crowd like Barry Sanders. The faster I move, the more my arms start to swing. When I zero in on the tall, blonde woman in front of me, I accidentally brush the back of my right hand against her left buttock. Now I can say I know what Paris Hilton's ass feels like. There's more junk in the trunk than I expected.

I'm paralyzed with fear. Damn my curiosity. Why did I have to come this way? I'm waiting for her to turn and cause a scene that's sure to make the papers. Harassment charges will be leveled, I'm sure. But Paris doesn't flinch. Maybe she's got Botox in those cheeks.

The Knicks win 98–88 and they're feeling good about the young season. Coach Lenny Wilkens likes the way Crawford is playing with Marbury in the backcourt. The Cavaliers are impressed as well. "He caught fire and was hitting everything," says Drew Gooden. "You could tell he was shooting good because he wasn't even following through. He was just tossing it up there. And I thought we were playing good D on him, too."

"Man, now I know the feeling everyone talks about," says Crawford. "This is what it's like to win. This is great. I don't ever want to lose this feeling."

The Knicks are 4–5. The dynasty is still a ways away but Jamal doesn't care. Neither does Paris.

LeBron emerges from the shower and, with one towel around his waist and another around his neck, slumps into the seat at his locker. "Man, I'm tired as fuck," he says. The Cavs' flight to New York arrived at 3 a.m. "I'm so motherfuckin' tired, can't even get dressed," he sighs. "I just want to go to sleep right here."

He asks Cavaliers PR person Amanda Mercado for a box score and looks it over. "Wait a minute," he says in mock anger. "How come you didn't tell me I was one rebound away from a triple double? Man, I could have had a fucking triple. You're supposed to tell me that."

Ten minutes later, he tells the media hoard huddled in the hallway outside that he could care less about his stats when the team is losing.

"C'mon, man, close that door," Drew Gooden calls out. "My balls are showing."

I do the honors so as not to disturb the LeBron Show.

"Hey, hey, you," LeBron says to one of my colleagues in the press. "Why do you keep leaning over people's shoulders? You eavesdropping or something?"

"No, I'm with *Cold Pizza*," the dude replies. He walks over and extends his hand. LeBron leaves him hanging without batting an eye.

"No thanks, I don't like cold pizza," he says. "I like my pizza warm."

The Cavs break out in laughter and egg him on.

"What is *Cold Pizza* anyway?" asks LeBron.

"It's ESPN's morning show. You want to be on? It airs from 8 to 10 a.m."

"*Eight a.m.?* Pfff! You can forget that. I'ma be sleeping. Better get yourself a microwave!"

THE CORRIDOR OUTSIDE THE Garden's locker rooms is hallowed ground. People in New York call it the Tunnel. This is where the NBA's hoi polloi—league officials, celebrities, and friends of the players—congregate after each game. The bigger the game, the bigger the names. Willis Reed limped through this passageway onto center court before Game Seven of the 1970 NBA Finals. As I make my way to the Knicks locker room, I scan the floor for footprints, half thinking I might spot Reed's Converse imprints outlining the famous toepath traveled by Frank Sinatra, Muhammad Ali and Bob Dylan. But my eyes only lead me to the shiny black dress shoes of Jamal Crawford.

"Yo, J.C., over here," I say when at last he appears.

"I didn't know you were here," he says.

"Yeah, man, remember the book idea I talked to you about? I just want to make sure you're totally on board for it."

"Did you talk to Aaron?" he asks.

That's not what I expected him to say.

Along with Crawford and Dwight Howard, Aaron Goodwin represents a dozen or so of the league's biggest names, not to mention the very biggest: LeBron James. That's trouble. Goodwin doesn't exactly see eye-to-eye with *The Magazine* — not since my colleague Tom Friend wrote a profile on LeBron in his senior year of high school. Friend didn't get his facts wrong but LeBron felt he portrayed his mother, Gloria, in an unfavorable light. From that day forward, LeBron put *The Magazine* on his banned substance list.

Crawford is one of my favorite players in the league. Always engaging and generous with his time, he never thinks about letting me pick up a dinner check and once — though I futilely resisted — he even paid for the gas in my car with his credit card. We have similar interests: music, the life of Tupac Shakur, and basketball. Behind closed doors, Crawford isn't afraid to talk candidly. He trusts me to separate what's fit to print from what's "off the record" without having to acknowledge it every five seconds.

"So just talk to Aaron and make sure he's cool with it," Crawford says.

He won't be. I'm doomed. I know it.

Aaron Goodwin ranks No. 8 on *Sports Illustrated's* list of the most influential minorities in sports. He's negotiated more than $135 million worth of endorsement contracts for LeBron alone — including a $90 million agreement with Nike. Thanks to Goodwin, LeBron is a pitchman for two Coca-Cola brands: Sprite and POWERade.

Goodwin grew up in East Oakland, California, where he attended the high school games of a young guard named Gary Payton. He got his start in the business with California Diversified Enterprises in 1987. Over the years, he's worked hard to build relationships with the families of promising young high school players, a practice that's widely viewed in amateur athletic circles as overly opportunistic. Payton hired him right out of Oregon State in 1990. Jason Kidd and Damon Stoudamire soon followed.

Goodwin is fiercely loyal to his players. He's ruffled more than a few front-office feathers to ensure that his clients' needs are met. When Kidd conflicted with teammate Jim Jackson in Dallas in 1996, Goodwin publicly proclaimed that it might be time for Kidd to move on. Two weeks later, he was traded to Phoenix.

Goodwin's clients appreciate the novelty of finding an agent who's wary of self-promotion. "I'm fiercely protective of my privacy and fiercely protective to my players," the agent told *The Seattle Times* in 2003. "I don't want to use the media as a billboard. I'll talk to the families face-to-face. That's where they'll get to know me. And I'm going to continue to do it that way. I'm not going to do TV just to get my name out there. That's not sincere."

In short, Goodwin prides himself on protecting his clients' interests, and his main client isn't interested in talking to a writer from *The Magazine*.

Goodwin has never met me. Nor has his partner and twin brother, Eric. They only know that I write for The Enemy. *First Dwight Howard, now Crawford. How am I going to beat the house with my shaky hand? This is bad. Oh… so… very… shit.*

With Crawford standing in front of me, I make an appeal to our friendship.

"You should have heard what Drew Gooden said about you," I say.

Crawford looks over my shoulder to the person standing behind me.

"What?" he says, waving his hand above my head. "Call me in a couple hours. Tell me about it tonight."

He walks past me to Aaron Goodwin and wraps him in a hug. Goodwin congratulates him on the Knicks' big win. Crawford smiles ear to ear.

GLENN DALE, MARYLAND, NOVEMBER 25

I'M EXHAUSTED. THREE WEEKS into the season, little has worked out. But over Thanksgiving dinner at my parents' home, I reassure myself that things will change. Before leaving for Los Angeles, I sit on a small bench in my father's garden and say a little prayer. *Please, God, help me to nail down commitments from Jamal Crawford and Dwight Howard.* I forget to mention Baron Davis.

LOS ANGELES, NOVEMBER 28

THE CLIPPERS AND WARRIORS are caught up in a yawner—no other way to put it. I spend most of the game scribbling notes on what to say to Davis' agent, Todd Ramasar, when I get him on the phone. The rest of the time I eyeball the Clippers' Spirit Dance Team, exchanging glances with a perky brunette with shoulder-length hair. Between routines, she waits by the exit next to press row. After bouncing onto the court to dance up a storm to Britney's "Toxic," she flashes me a smile—half seductive, half Go Team!

Cheerleaders are forbidden to fraternize with players. As far as I know, that restriction doesn't apply to young writers. I'd be stupid not to make a move, but I have to focus. I'm here to hook up with Elton Brand. Mr. Reliable, like a John Deere tractor with a jumphook.

The Clippers emerge with a 103–91 triumph and I hustle to the locker room to make my pitch. "I see us meeting up about once a month," I say. "On the road, here in L.A., wherever the schedule finds us."

"That's a plan," Brand replies. "This is going to be good. Don't worry about a thing—we'll do this right."

See what I mean? The guy's a rock, super dependable, as I once heard Coach K say.

Feeling empowered, I return to the court, climb the stairs, and head for the exit near the statue of Magic Johnson leading the break. Hanging a hard right without looking, I smash into a woman who has parked herself in front of the restrooms—directly in my path. My notebook and game notes go flying. "Excuse me, miss," I say, bending down to pick them up. The battery has popped out of my cell phone and I can't seem to squeeze it back in. "I'm sorry, miss, I didn't see you," I stammer.

And why am I calling her miss?

"Get a good look at the cheerleaders?" she asks.

Boy is my face red.

"What's that?"

"Weren't you sitting across from the cheerleaders?"

"Nah, I was checking my, um, surroundings."

When in doubt, change the subject. My eyes dart to the yellow-rhinestone-studded cell phone tucked into her low rider jeans.

"Whataya go to UCLA or something?"

"No, I work for an ad agency in L.A. Well, our offices are actually in Santa Monica."

"I'm Chris."

"Nicole. My friend's in the bathroom."

Dirty blonde hair, cute smile, exposed hips, and stylish heels. Hotness personified. Keep her talking—I've got to think of a way to ask for her phone number.

"Are you a Clippers fan?"

"No, I don't really like basketball. I got the company tickets because my boss is skiing in Aspen this weekend."

"No way, Aspen? Colorado, right?"

"Have you been there?"

"Not recently."

Or ever.

"I don't ski but I'm going to learn to surf. I just got a surfboard," she says.

"Really? I'm saving up for a boogie board."

She laughs.

It's now or never.

"I actually have to go but we should exchange information."

"Sure, yeah," she says.

…and I don't see a gun to her head.

I pop the battery back into my cell phone and anxiously wait for it to power up. There's a lull in the conversation. I'm completely out of material. We say our goodbyes and I promise to call her. I like to give people nicknames when I add them to my phone list. I punch her in as Miss Nikki.

When I pass the statue outside the Staples Center, I'm feeling it. "You should've seen me, Magic," I say.

Confidence is high. I repeat, confidence is high.

LOS ANGELES, NOVEMBER 29

ONE PLAYER DOWN, FOUR to go. Dwyane Wade's agent called me after the Clippers game to tell me the project's not right for his client—he's too private—but Dwyane wishes me luck. Carmelo Anthony has passed, too. His off-season was a public relations disaster. His reps want no part of me or the book. Baron Davis, Jamal Crawford and Dwight Howard haven't said no, but I can't keep following them indefinitely. I need to know where we stand—and soon. Last night, I returned to Staples for the Lakers, 6:30 p.m. matchup with the 1–11 Hornets. After the game, I cornered Baron in the hallway outside the locker room.

"Man, we need a win," he said.

And the award for understatement of the year goes to...the envelope, please...Baron Davis!

This morning, I awake in my hotel room to the sound of a cell phone buzzing. Davis' agent, Todd Ramasar, is on the line. He and Davis went to UCLA together. Now Ramasar is an upwardly mobile jet setter in Baron's crew, just like hip-hop star The Game, former high school teammate and assistant film producer Cash Warren, who dates Jessica Alba, and Dart Stamps, Baron's trainer and former AAU coach.

Ramasar's no Goodwin. For that, I'm glad.

"I'm calling to tell you we're going to pass on the book," he says. "Baron loves the idea but he's got some other things going on right now."

"Okay" I tell him. "Thanks for your interest."

I hang up the phone and sit on the edge of the bed. I don't have the slightest interest in pleading with him. What can I say? The Hornets are speeding toward the wrong kind of history.

EASTERN CONFERENCE

ATLANTIC DIVISION

	W	L	PCT	GB	HOME	ROAD	LAST—10	STREAK
New York	7	6	.538	—	5—1	2—5	6—4	Won 2
Philadelphia	6	7	.462	1	5—3	1—4	5—5	Lost 1
Toronto	7	9	.437	1.5	5—2	2—7	3—7	Won 1
Boston	5	8	.385	2	3—4	2—4	4—6	Won 1
New Jersey	3	11	.214	4.5	2—6	1—5	1—9	Won 1

CENTRAL DIVISION

	W	L	PCT	GB	HOME	ROAD	LAST—10	STREAK
Indiana	10	4	.714	—	6—2	4—2	6—4	Lost 1
Cleveland	9	5	.643	1	6—1	3—4	8—2	Lost 1
Detroit	7	7	.500	3	5—1	2—6	4—6	Won 1
Milwaukee	4	8	.333	5	4—2	0—6	3—7	Lost 1
Chicago	1	10	.091	7.5	0—3	1—7	1—9	Lost 1

SOUTHEAST DIVISION

	W	L	PCT	GB	HOME	ROAD	LAST—10	STREAK
Miami	10	6	.625	—	6—3	4—3	6—4	Lost 1
Orlando	8	5	.615	0.5	5—2	3—3	6—4	Lost 1
Washington	7	5	.583	1	3—2	4—3	5—5	Won 1
Charlotte	3	10	.231	5.5	3—4	0—6	2—8	Lost 1
Atlanta	2	12	.143	7	1—6	1—6	2—8	Lost 7

WESTERN CONFERENCE

SOUTHWEST DIVISION

	W	L	PCT	GB	HOME	ROAD	LAST—10	STREAK
San Antonio	12	3	.800	—	6—0	6—3	8—2	Won 4
Dallas	10	6	.625	2.5	5—3	5—3	5—5	Lost 1
Houston	6	10	.375	6.5	2—5	4—5	3—7	Lost 4
Memphis	5	10	.333	7	3—5	2—5	4—6	Lost 4
New Orleans	1	12	.077	10	0—6	1—6	1—9	Lost 4

NORTHWEST DIVISION

	W	L	PCT	GB	HOME	ROAD	LAST—10	STREAK
Seattle	13	3	.812	—	7—0	6—3	8—2	Lost 1
Minnesota	8	5	.615	3.5	4—2	4—3	6—4	Won 2
Denver	8	6	.571	4	7—3	1—3	7—3	Won 2
Portland	8	6	.571	4	5—2	3—4	6—4	Won 2
Utah	8	7	.533	4.5	4—4	4—3	4—6	Lost 2

PACIFIC DIVISION

	W	L	PCT	GB	HOME	ROAD	LAST—10	STREAK
Phoenix	12	2	.857	—	5—1	7—1	8—2	Won 8
Sacramento	9	5	.643	3	6—1	3—4	8—2	Won 1
L.A. Clippers	9	6	.600	3.5	5—3	4—3	6—4	Won 4
L.A. Lakers	9	6	.600	3.5	6—2	3—4	6—4	Won 2
Golden State	3	10	.231	8.5	2—5	1—5	3—7	Lost 2

"CALL MY AGENT"

NEW YORK, DECEMBER 1

AFTER FLASHING MY MEDIA badge at the green-jacketed security guard, I enter the tunnel. For some reason, the staff at Madison Square Garden just loves to see my credentials. Something about me must shout menace. Maybe it's the backwards hat or the Rocawears. Whatever. At least Jay Williams is happy to see me.

"Yo, Jay," I say, giving him a pound, "What's up, son?"

"Aw, shit, what up, Chris?" comes the reply. "You know the only thing I'm up to—gettin' back. You ain't even got to ask me that."

"You dunking yet?"

"Off the vert. You know I got to keep my shit sexy. For real."

He was one of the most gifted athletes in the game—the No. 2 pick in the 2002 draft—but in June of 2003, after a promising rookie season, Williams nearly died in a motorcycle accident. On the way to dinner with a friend, he revved his red-and-black Yamaha R6 into a telephone pole, fracturing his pelvis and destroying ligaments and a nerve in his left leg. Doctors briefly pondered amputation.

Were it not for that singular indiscretion, he might well be riding high atop the league. The successor to Jason Kidd. Two years away from a big payday. Instead, he suffers miserably each time he enters an arena. The pain of thinking what might have been.

It's not as though his life is awful. He has collected more than $4 million from the three-year guaranteed contract he signed with the Bulls. He's got a beautiful girlfriend and loving parents who check on him daily. And, of course, he has his health. But despite eighteen months of intensive rehab, he will likely never attain what he desires most, the dream he pursued with such vigor.

Getting on with your life isn't so bad when you've never tasted life in the league. Like most kids who played basketball, I too dreamed of playing in the NBA. But the day I realized I couldn't cut it, no one cried. My downfall had nothing to do with tragedy and everything to do with statistics. I had enough hops to throw down a highlight dunk every now and again, but I never had the talent to attract a major college program. I just wasn't good enough. The dream died during my junior year at Howard University, the day I was cut trying to walk on to the men's team. After I left the coach's office, I sat on the steps outside Burr Gymnasium and cried.

In the end, discovering that I wasn't good enough to make one of the worst teams in college hoops was a relief. It takes a lot of energy to fool yourself into believing the impossible. I can only imagine how much harder it would have been for me to accept the truth if I were, like Williams, a star at Duke, a man who had tasted the sweet nectar of success in the NBA. Wouldn't I do everything in my power to get it back—even if the odds were overwhelmingly against me?

It's funny how many guys cling to their false hopes long after they're gone. Like me, they see windows of opportunity in the thickest of brick walls. Jay never needed a window. He was that good. But he sure as hell could use an opening now.

"I'm so focused it's not even funny," he says. "I want this so bad—more than I wanted to get into the league in the first place."

We walk the hall to the Knicks locker room side by side. I search for something profound to say. I got nothing. Penny Hardaway breaks the awkward silence by bursting out of the locker room. He greets Williams, offering wisdom and solace all at once. "Be patient," he says. "It'll come. You can be sure. You'll be back."

"Thanks man. That means a lot."

Stephon Marbury lifts Williams' spirits on the other side of the door, draped in a towel, his torso beaded with drops of water. "J Wizzy— it's you!" he shouts. "How you feel, playa?"

"Good. I'm doin' it the best I can, you know?"

Then Williams spots Jamal Crawford in the corner. When Crawford looks up, his mouth drops. He hasn't seen Jay in over a year.

Three seasons ago, Crawford was a confused young point guard. He hated playing for the Bulls' inexperienced coach, Tim Floyd, and he was certain the feeling was mutual. Then when Bill Cartwright replaced Floyd, Crawford found himself in a bitter power struggle with his boyhood idol Jalen Rose. John Paxson, the team's general manager, called Crawford into his office for a talk. He told him how much he loved his game. But, after assuring him and reassuring him that he was the man, Paxson went ahead and drafted Williams with the No. 2 pick.

Now young players will tell you they understand how the league works— "I know this is a business…" —but the cold, hard reality of it kills them every time. When their names scroll across the bottom of the TV screen as the result of some transaction, they call their parents in tears.

Crawford was pissed—and scared. Early the next season, he rushed home to Seattle to attend to his ailing grandmother, missing a prime-time showdown with Jason Kidd of the Nets. As Crawford watched on television, Williams racked up 26 points, 13 assists, and

14 rebounds in his place—a line unmatched by any rookie since (including LeBron James). When Crawford returned to the team a few days later, the two players were on opposite sides of a continental divide. They were so physical when guarding each other in practice, they had to be separated.

By March, the Bulls were just dreadful and management started playing one guard off the other. Crawford couldn't take it. He approached Willams. They had a talk. Everything came out. They agreed to end the stalemate. They started talking on the phone, visiting each other's homes. By season's end, no two Bulls were tighter. Two months later, Williams wrecked his motorcycle.

When Crawford sees him in the lockerroom, Williams might as well be a ghost.

"Tell me what you've been up to," Crawford says.

"Just working out, man. I'm trying to get back where I was."

"I heard you bought a house. Your mom still living with you?"

"Hell nah! I'm a grown-ass man!"

They laugh in a way that only two NBA players can. To get the joke, you've got to be inside the rope. For a few special moments, Jay Williams is one of the boys again. Back in the league.

"All right," he says. "I'ma get on out of here and let you do your media thing."

They hug. Jamal makes sure Jay has his latest telephone number. He's notorious among his peers for changing his digits.

"Hit me up," Jay says.

"For sure, for sure," Jamal replies.

Williams departs and I suddenly remember that I want to talk to him in Chicago next week about Bulls rookie Luol Deng. I jet from the locker room. When I step into the hallway, he's nowhere in sight.

Yep, it kills him to be here—on the outside looking in.

CHICAGO, DECEMBER 7

I PULL UP IN front of the gated community in Deerfield, Illinois, ten minutes south of the Bulls' practice facility. Since August, Luol Deng has called this home. His agent chose this location for his client because it's like an active community for under-25 lottery picks. Teammates Tyson Chandler, Ben Gordon, and Eddy Curry are local residents, too.

At first glance, the houses look like mansions, but on closer inspection, they appear to be townhouses glued together by the location scout for *MTV Cribs*. I'm sitting in a fire lane outside the entrance, waiting for Deng's manager, Josh Nochimson. He's arranged for Deng, fellow rookie Chris Duhon, and me to attend an awards banquet in honor of the 5–11 Chicago Bears. To kill time, I leave yet another message on Aaron Goodwin's cell phone. That makes seven in the last twelve days.

The security guard in the booth is eyeballing me something fierce. After a few minutes, he ambles toward the car with flashlight in hand.

"Can I help you?"

"I'm waiting for a resident of the complex," I say.

"Who?"

"Deng. Luol."

"Can you do me a favor and shut the engine off?"

He returns to the booth and I go back to waiting.

Man, I hate this. As the minutes tick off the digital dashboard clock, I start to get antsy. I think I spot Nochimson in every car I see, and I swear like forty cars have passed in the last twenty minutes. I hunker down and roll with it because waiting is a huge part of my job. Nobody told me this when I raised my hand at the high school job fair, but when you deal with professional athletes, you best be prepared to spend the day waiting. Waiting for them to get dressed, to show up, to finish shooting free throws, to do an interview, to get a massage, to hang up the phone, to get on the ball. Whatever. Waiting, waiting, and more waiting.

Wait a minute, I think I see Nochimson. A white Chevy Blazer pulls up beside me and down comes the passenger-side window.

"What's up? Been waiting long?"

"Nah, just got here."

"Good. Follow me."

Several quick lefts and a few rights later, we end up at Deng's crib. Forward Andres Nocioni lives next door. The two rookies bonded instantly at training camp. Deng, a native of Sudan, looks up to the 25-year-old Argentinian because he had a few years of professional basketball experience in Europe. Now, with their houses joined, they can literally check up on each other by banging on the wall.

Deng paces the kitchen in his socks, talking on a portable phone to his brother, Ajou, a former center at Fairfield University. Dale Walker his personal chef, sits on the steps in the hallway. Nochimson has arranged for Walker, who lives in Detroit, to stay ten minutes away during the season in a spanking new $350,000 three-story townhouse. Walker cooks breakfast every morning for Deng and his best friend and roommate Adam Andre closely monitoring their diets.

A few weeks back, Andre and Deng got the current must-have toy among NBA types: the Sidekick II two-way cell phone/pager. They seem to enjoy fiddling with the flip-up screens and the Internet access more than they do actually making calls. The laptop in the living room sports a never-ending slide show featuring Andre's favorite sex symbol, Paris Hilton. No doubt about it, this is one fine set-up, albeit a supervised set-up. Rare is the moment when Andre and Deng escape the watchful eyes of their handlers: Nochimson, his business partner Kevin Bradbury, and Walker. "We want Louie to survive his rookie season," says Nochimson.

Fifteen minutes later, Deng, Andre and I jump in Deng's 2005 Range Rover and follow Nochimson and Walker down I-94 for a traffic-congested ride into downtown Chicago. We pass a billboard offering Bulls season ticket plans with the team marketing slogan plastered on it in red letters: THROUGH THICK AND THIN.

Deng reads the billboard aloud.

"What does this mean?" he asks. "What is this thick and thin?"

"Good times and bad," I tell him from the back seat.

"Man, we been thin for a minute, huh?"

"Yeah, 354-losses-since-M.J. thin."

"How do you know that?"

"Research, young fella."

Andre's cell phone rings. He looks at the caller I.D. and sees that it's his mom, Nancy, calling from back home in New Jersey. She too phones nearly every day to check on the boys. Deng grabs the cell from Andre's right hand and answers it in his best impersonation of a nasally white boy.

"Hello this is Adam…your son…seriously it's me…*seriously*… don't you recognize your own son?"

Embarrassed, Andre shakes his head and tries to suppress a laugh. Deng reverts to his Baskin-Robbins-sweet voice and greets Nancy as if she were his own mother. In a way, she is.

Deng was born to a wealthy Dinka family in Sudan in 1985. His father, Aldo, was an elected official who served for twenty-two years in various state roles, including provincial governor, deputy speaker, and deputy prime minister. As permitted by Dinka law, Aldo had three wives and sixteen children. Luol was the eighth of nine born to his mother, Martha.

In 1989, when Luol was 4 years old, the Sudanese government was overthrown and, like many in office, Aldo was sent to jail. He was released four months later on the condition that he help negotiate peace between the Christian south and Muslim north. He packed up his family instead and, leaving most of the Dengs' worldly possessions behind, fled to Egypt's Mediterranean coast. Luol lived with his mother and eight siblings in a cramped three-bedroom apartment. They were fed by a local church group. On December 15, 1993, Aldo moved to London with Martha and asked for political asylum. A few weeks later, the children joined them in government-sponsored housing in London's south side, marveling at the modern cars, the appliances, and the television sets. They spoke a mixture of Dinka and Arabic, but virtually no English. Luol picked up the language quickly, gamely enduring the ribbing, from his brothers, who were amused by his new accent.

He spent his early teens at the Brixton Recreation Centre, playing soccer and basketball for the Brixton Topcats. He became a devoted Arsenal fan, putting a poster of Ian Wright on his wall. But by the age of 14, his wiry frame stretched to 6-foot-5 and his days on the pitch were numbered. Years earlier, while shooting hoops at a court in Alexandria, Egypt, Luol and his older brother Ajou were spotted by Manute Bol, a fellow Dinka who played in the NBA. The vacationing pro stopped to give the boys some instruction. When he learned of the family's plight, he befriended the Dengs and did his best to keep tabs on them.

In 1997, Ajou caught the eye of University of Connecticut coach Jim Calhoun who offered him a scholarship. Two years later, Luol led England's 15-and-under basketball team to the finals of the European junior tournament in Poland. His sister Arek played for England's girls' team. Both received full scholarship offers from the Blair Academy in New Jersey, where Andre was a senior on the varsity team.

Luol moved in with the Andre family. He and Adam were like brothers. Whenever Luol missed his siblings and friends in Great Britain, Nancy talked him through it. Scarcely a day went by when she didn't ask him how he was feeling. She treated him like one of her own. When Adam went away to college, Luol inherited his chores.

In other words, there's no way Luol's going to fool her with a fake voice. A mother can always tell her sons apart.

When we pull up to the Hilton on Michigan Avenue, Nochimson and Walker are waiting for us in the lobby. The boys look sharp tonight. Deng wears gray slacks with perfect creases in them and a gray dress shirt that hangs a foot below his waist. Andre wears a similar-but-slightly-darker number. Standard issue for NBA rookies, these outfits are comfortable, casual, and professional all at the same time. They save you from wearing a jacket and can usually be snatched right off the rack at any big and tall store.

My black Gap lint-trap pants and burgundy-and-black striped shirt suddenly feel inappropriate. I find myself looking in the lobby mirrors, adjusting the tucked-in-ness of my shirt. Why can't I be smooth like these guys every now and then? I start to think that working out is the key. *Yeah, that way my clothes will fit better.* I guess what's really bothering me is that I forgot to pack shoes. Gray-on-black Nike Air Zoom Huarache hightops are the best I can do. I can't wait to sit down and hide them under the table.

We enter the ballroom and I flash back to prom night. There are tuxes and ballgowns everywhere I look. The space is cavernous. Every railing and picture frame is exquisitely carved. Elaborate chandeliers hang from the ceiling above. If Al Capone walked in, I wouldn't be surprised.

Thirty minutes before dinner, we check out the items in the silent auction: a Colts helmet autographed by Peyton Manning, a James

Gandolfini poster, and a Gale Sayers jersey. We take our table near the stage and listen politely as a handful of Bears address the guests. After their remarks, we wait quietly for the boneless chicken breast, mashed potatoes, and chocolate mousse. Deng stares straight ahead, zoning out. He can't wait for this to end.

The man in the chair next to him extends his hand.

"Hi, I'm Jerry Azumah," says the one-time Pro Bowl cornerback.

"I'm Luol Deng. Nice to meet you."

When at last we're excused from the table, we pass a table filled with goodie bags. Inside each one, we find an official NFL football with a white leather panel on it for autographs. Deng wraps his massive hand around the ball, nearly eclipsing the white panel and chucks it sidearm ten yards to me. As the pigskin sails back and forth, he starts to feel mighty confident in his ball control.

"You think I can toss it on that balcony?" he asks pointing Ruth-like to a spot far away. *This I gotta see.*

"There's no way in hell you can make that throw," I tell him. "In fact, I'll give you ten bucks if you chuck it up there."

His lips twist into a mischievous smile and he begins to cock his arm back *a la* Daunte Culpepper.

"Louie!"

Standing behind us with a look of horror on his face is Nochimson. "We're not paying for any chandeliers tonight," he says sternly.

Damn, almost made ten bucks.

MILWAUKEE, DECEMBER 8

IT'S LATE. I'M GOING to miss the opening tip for the Bucks and the Heat. My cell phone rings. It's Aaron Goodwin. I stare at the caller I.D. in amazement. I've been waiting for him to get back to me for weeks. I'm so stunned I don't notice the car drifting to the right—not until I'm heading straight for a concrete barrier. I grab the wheel hard, sending the tires screeching to the left and the poor old woman behind me into the path of a seventeen-ton truck. Lucky for both of us, the guy in the eighteen-wheeler is a much better driver. Otherwise there'd be serious carnage.

"Are you still there?" Goodwin asks. "Hello?"

"Yes Aaron I'm here."

My voice is shaky. I've got the cell phone pressed to my ear and my right hand applying a death grip to the wheel. My heart's racing. I manage to take a deep breath before I launch into an unrehearsed, rambling spiel about how great this book will be for his clients. I'm angry with myself for getting caught off guard. I'm killing my chances for a yes.

"Can you hold on for a quick second?" I ask. "Gotta pay the parking lot attendant."

I veer off the highway five blocks from the garage. In the driveway of a construction lot, I take a moment to compose myself. For the next few minutes, I speak without a breath about the unique benefits of my book project. No way he can say no to me now. "Man, you can't buy this kind of pub," I tell him. "It's going to be a great story."

"Yeah, but I know how editors like to go in and change things," he says.

"That can't happen," I counter. "My contract says I have final approval of all copy. Nothing gets in there unless I say the word."

He loosens up a bit.

"So what kind of things are you going to talk about in the book?"

"Life. Everything players experience over the course of a season. What it's really like to play in the league."

"That can only hurt my clients," Goodwin answers sharply.

"Why? How? Are they into illegal activity? Come on, this isn't an expose on why the league can't be saved by some crusty-ass writer from *Sports Illustrated!*"

All quiet on the other end. He's thinking. If only I were talking to him in person, I'd close this deal. I'm sure of it.

"Look, I'm on your side," I say. "The players know me. I'm not that far removed from playing AAU ball and going to summer camps myself."

Another pause.

"OK," he says. "I'll talk to Jamal, but not Dwight. We're documenting his rookie year so he can do his own book someday."

"Then I'll go with Jamal."

"Let me call him and I'll get back to you."

"That sounds great, Aaron. Thanks a lot."

That's the last time I hear from him.

NEW YORK, DECEMBER 15

TRADE RUMORS ARE WEIGHING heavy on Jamal Crawford's mind. Vince Carter wants out of Toronto and Isiah Thomas is hypnotized by the idea of having the one-time "Greatest Show on Earth" in New York by February's All-Star break. More frustrating still, the rumors have surfaced during a hot streak. In his last two games, Crawford has scored 30 points against the Nets and 31 against the Nuggets. Tonight at the Garden, he'll match up against Richard Hamilton, one of the purest shooters in the league.

I've been thinking about changing two-guards myself. I don't know if I can count on Crawford much longer and Hamilton plays for the World Champion Detroit Pistons. All the guy does is win. In 1999, he was the Most Outstanding Player on the 34–2 University of Connecticut team that won the national championship. Now he's got an NBA ring to match. The sixth-year veteran is living every kid's dream.

Why not let the two players duke it out on the court? The 10–10 Pistons are off to a horrible start as the defending champs. They're coming off embarrassing losses to Memphis and Atlanta. The team's inconsistency is eating away at head coach Larry Brown. A year ago, his boys snuck up on the NBA, overwhelming their opponents with grit and passion. This season, they're playing like zombies.

Crawford is another story. Perhaps you've heard the tale about the guy who misses nine straight shots but bets the farm he'll hit number ten? That's him. When he's on, he doesn't even have to look at the rim. Tonight the arc on his rainbow twenty-five footers is as beautiful as anything you'll find in nature. He's drilled four treys in the first quarter. As the buzzer sounds on the first half, he pops in a fifth from twenty-six feet out to give the Knicks a 56–40 lead.

In the second half, the Pistons come to life. The Knicks can't buy a clean look at the hoop. With every steal, every rebound, Detroit is off and running. Chauncey Billups nails two free throws with 2.6 seconds to go to seal a 94–93 victory. In forty-eight minutes of play, the Pistons lead for forty-two seconds.

By the time I find Crawford in the locker room, I've worked up a good head of steam. I don't care one lick about the game. I just want to know one thing: Is he in or out? It's December for Havlicek's sake! I'm tired of getting the runaround.

"Yo, I talked to Aaron about the book project," I say. "He seemed pretty comfortable and said he was going to speak to you about it. Have you talked to him?"

"Nah, he didn't mention anything to me."

"I can't picture this book without you. Do you want to do it?"

"Yeah," he says, with a distinct lack of enthusiasm. "Call me tonight."

I do. I'm still waiting for a call back.

I've been let down by athletes before. It's part of the job. Three summers ago, the clothing company AND1 invited me to watch Kevin Garnett film a commercial. It was one of those day-in-the-life deals. "Write whatever you see," the AND1 flack told me. Two months earlier, Garnett's Timberwolves had been bounced from the first round of the playoffs for the sixth year in a row. People were beginning to question his fortitude, treating him like a six-year, $125 million piñata.

The AND1 commercial was set in a dingy interrogation room. The whole thing was loosely scripted. The director tossed out questions. Garnett winged back answers. "This is real," he said afterwards. "This is the real K.G."

Q: Are you overpaid?

K.G.: Hell no. If anything, I'm underpaid with everything I do. That's a ridiculous question. I have to do everything for this team.

Q: Are you tough enough to play in the Western Conference? Maybe Minnesota should move to the East?

K.G.: Man, I've been in the Western Conference for seven years. Holdin' it down. Nobody there scares me. Look at my numbers. You know my rap sheet.

Q: What are your numbers?

KG: Twenty, ten and five. Twenty, ten and five. Three years in a row. And I'm rounding down. Who else has done that?

Q: What does that get you?

K.G.: It gets you what it gets you.

Q: Does it get you out of the first round?
K.G.: We'll get out of the first round when everybody does their part. Players, coaches, management, everybody. I can't do everything by myself. It'll get us past the first round if motherfuckers do their part.

Q: Word on the street is that you're soft in the fourth quarter.
K.G.: Fuck you talkin' about? That's not what I hear.

Q: What do you hear?
K.G.: That K.G. is the motherfucking shit. Niggas know. My peers in the league know what I'm about.

Q: What have you learned about the fourth quarter?
K.G.: To not pass the ball if we're losing.

After the shoot, we went to dinner in downtown Minneapolis. The manager at Ruth's Chris Steak House kept the kitchen open after hours for Garnett and his boys. They never had to pay for a meal. That night, Garnett revealed the softer side of his personality as well. He was funny, thoughtful, sincere, and revealing.

I was proud of the piece I wrote afterwards. For a young reporter, it was a real feather in my cap. The day after the story ran on ESPN.com, I appeared live on the 6 o'clock *SportsCenter*. I made my way to the TV studio in the ESPN Zone in Times Square ready to tell the world that Kevin Garnett was poised to turn things around. The anchor interviewed me for several minutes. As I left the Zone, my cell phone was buzzing like crazy. Old coaches and former girlfriends and guys from the grocery store where I used to stock shelves called to congratulate me. They were all happy for me.

Not Garnett. He was so pissed off he went to a TV studio in mid-town Manhattan to be interviewed via satellite by ESPN's Dan Patrick. When I got home and turned on the 11 o'clock *SportsCenter*, I heard the following tease: "Reporter and player disagree over story." The network broadcast a clip of me saying something about K.G., then, shockingly, a clip of him denying it. "Holy shit!" I screamed.

Fidgeting like a kindergartener with ADD, he categorically denied everything. The commercial was scripted, he said. He was acting. I was a reporter trying to make a name for myself.

The AND1 people saw everything I did. They were so apologetic, they offered to rent me a Ferrari Spider just like Garnett's for one month—an offer I refused. I felt disillusioned, but Kevin Garnett was simply an interview subject so his betrayal didn't haunt me for long. Crawford and I are so tight that his snub cuts me to the core. Not because he doesn't want to do the book. I'm fine with that. Not because he wants to consult his agent. I'm fine with that, too. But because he won't level with me as a friend.

We have not spoken since.

DETROIT, DECEMER 18

IN NASCAR, IT'S CALLED drafting. Riding the rear bumper of the car in front of you so that your vehicle gets pulled along in the slipstream. At 190 miles per hour, it's highly effective. But it can be equally effective at, say, walking speed...in the bowels of the Palace...when Kid Rock and his crew are about to enter the Pistons' locker room. The door is closed to the press for another five minutes, but Kid Rock is a celebrity so he gets a free pass. And by attaching myself to the back of his crew, so do I—just like Daytona, yo.

Clutching a Pabst and wearing a Kid Rock jersey, the pop star steps inside and starts addressing the Pistons by their first names. "When you gonna pimp my ride like one of yours?" Lindsey Hunter asks him. "Seriously, when?" Tayshaun Prince inquires about motorcycles. Kid spies the forty-two-inch flat-screen TV broadcasting the Suns game. "Oh, Steve Nash, that's my boy," he says. "I love that longhaired freak. He's got my kind of game."

Next he reaches out to Chauncey Billups. "Hey, Chauncey, hook me up with a jersey, man. It's for my boy."

"I'll take care of you. I won't forget," Billups replies.

Derrick Coleman plops down at his locker. "D.C., how you been, baby?" Kid asks.

"Doing my thing. What about you?"

"Just living in the country and hunting," Kid says. "I'm using muskets since they outlawed fucking shotguns."

"Let's see what happens when you run up on a fucking twelve-pointer ready to run you ass over."

"Shit, I ain't worried about no deer. I'm hunting bears now. Fuck yeah, I am."

Kid's phone starts to blow up. His ring tone is Fabolous's "Breathe." "Time to go," he says. "They're waiting around back with the car."

DETROIT, DECEMBER 19

PRACTICE OFFICIALLY ENDED A half-hour ago and yet here is Larry Brown, standing at the top of the key, instructing his players on the fundamentals of one-on-one defense. Chauncey Billups pops out on the left wing and catches a pass from the coach. Richard Hamilton presses up on him. The moment Billups is about to make his move, Brown screams, "Stop!"

The 64-year-old coach walks over and nudges the inside of Hamilton's foot, coaxing him to spread his stance. "Get your arms out," he says. "Don't give him any options."

Billups drives the left baseline, spinning back to the right to launch a fadeaway jumper. Hamilton's skinny arm shoots out, grazing the ball. "Piece!" he shouts.

"Good job, Rip, that's what I want," cheers Brown.

This is how the World Champion Detroit Pistons close each practice. After a disappointing 12–11 start, they're trying to rekindle the intensity that leveled the Lakers in last year's Finals.

Not long ago, with Ben Wallace out of the lineup for six games due to his role in the November brawl, they were giving up 90.7 points a game. But, thanks to drills like this one, they've held their last five opponents to an average of 79.4.

Defense is only half the problem. On offense, the Pistons rank 28th in the league in scoring, 28th in field goal percentage and 25th in three-point percentage. The team's best post threat, Rasheed Wallace, has taken to shooting long-range jumpers. Detroit's ball movement—a point of pride in the playoffs—is way out of sync. "We don't have anyone who can drive and kick and create for others and it's really hurt us," Brown says. "Our shot selection has been terrible."

The lone ray of hope is the team's character. After hitting only 3 of 22 attempts against Portland on the worst night of his career, Hamilton simply cracks a smile. "I'm a shooter," he says, through his toothy grin. "I always think the next one's going in."

Of last month's brawl, Hamilton says, "We're determined not to use what happened against Indiana as an excuse. If you ask anybody on this team, they'll tell you we're past it." Looking around the gym, it's hard to argue with him. The mood is light-hearted, no different than the temperament that the Pistons displayed on their surprise title run last season. Nearly every player stays late to work on his game. Those who aren't shooting congregate under a side basket where Lindsey Hunter holds court. Their smiles and laughter belie the weeks of turbulence. Title defenses are *supposed* to be hard, Darvin Ham tells you.

Following another one of Brown's defensive clinics, Ben Wallace remains behind on the court. After tossing up a series of shots, he spots up behind the corner three—a good foot out of bounds. He releases a shot that crashes into the rim. The next one is an airball. The third hits the side of backboard. On his 11th shot, he holds the release a touch higher and bit longer. The ball swishes through the net. He turns and winks.

"I knew I'd get it back," he says. So does the team.

NEW YORK, DECEMBER 20

BACK IN MANHATTAN TO powwow with my editors, I file a couple of months' worth of expense reports and stock up on clean underwear. At long last, my roster is rounding into shape. At shooting guard I've got Richard Hamilton—the defending champ. Down low, two swingmen: Luol Deng, the rookie from Sudan, and Tracy McGrady, the superstar in need of a ring. At center I'll play power forward Elton Brand—the handyman struggling to make the Clippers respectable. That just leaves the point, and I've got the perfect candidate for the job. Damon Jones of Miami. It's high time someone gave him a chance.

Me? I'm the dorky sixth man trying to keep up with them all.

I like it.

EASTERN CONFERENCE

ATLANTIC DIVISION

	W	L	PCT	GB	HOME	ROAD	LAST—10	STREAK
New York	16	13	.552	—	10—4	6—9	7—3	Won 3
Philadelphia	13	15	.464	2.5	7—6	6—9	7—3	Lost 1
Boston	13	16	.448	3	8—5	5—11	5—5	Won 1
New Jersey	10	18	.357	5.5	6—8	4—10	5—5	Lost 1
Toronto	10	21	.323	7	8—4	2—17	3—7	Lost 3

CENTRAL DIVISION

	W	L	PCT	GB	HOME	ROAD	LAST—10	STREAK
Cleveland	17	12	.586	—	11—3	6—9	5—5	Lost 1
Detroit	15	13	.536	1.5	8—5	7—8	5—5	Lost 1
Indiana	15	13	.536	1.5	8—6	7—7	5—5	Won 3
Chicago	9	17	.346	6.5	6—8	3—9	6—4	Lost 2
Milwaukee	9	17	.346	6.5	7—7	2—10	4—6	Lost 1

SOUTHEAST DIVISION

	W	L	PCT	GB	HOME	ROAD	LAST—10	STREAK
Miami	24	7	.774	—	12—3	12—4	10—0	Won 13
Orlando	15	12	.556	7	9—4	6—8	4—6	Lost 2
Washington	15	13	.536	7.5	8—5	7—8	3—7	Lost 2
Charlotte	7	19	.269	14.5	6—7	1—12	3—7	Lost 4
Atlanta	5	23	.179	17.5	3—13	2—10	2—8	Lost 3

WESTERN CONFERENCE

SOUTHWEST DIVISION

	W	L	PCT	GB	HOME	ROAD	LAST—10	STREAK
San Antonio	25	6	.806	—	14—1	11—5	9—1	Won 5
Dallas	19	10	.655	5	9—6	10—4	7—3	Won 2
Houston	15	15	.500	9.5	10—7	5—8	6—4	Won 2
Memphis	14	17	.452	11	9—7	5—10	6—4	Won 2
New Orleans	2	26	.071	21.5	1—11	1—15	1—9	Lost 7

NORTHWEST DIVISION

	W	L	PCT	GB	HOME	ROAD	LAST—10	STREAK
Seattle	22	6	.786	—	11—3	11—3	7—3	Won 2
Minnesota	16	11	.593	5.5	8—3	8—8	5—5	Lost 1
Denver	14	15	.483	8.5	10—6	4—9	2—8	Won 1
Portland	13	14	.481	8.5	7—5	6—9	4—6	Lost 2
Utah	11	19	.367	12	6—8	5—11	2—8	Lost 4

PACIFIC DIVISION

	W	L	PCT	GB	HOME	ROAD	LAST—10	STREAK
Phoenix	25	4	.862	—	13—2	12—2	9—1	Won 1
Sacramento	18	9	.667	6	11—4	7—5	6—4	Won 1
L.A. Lakers	15	12	.556	9	10—6	5—6	5—5	Won 1
L.A. Clippers	13	15	.464	11.5	9—8	4—7	2—8	Lost 1
Golden State	11	18	.379	14	8—8	3—10	6—4	Won 4

PLENTY TO PROVE

MIAMI, JANUARY 3, 2005

ON NOVEMBER 30, 1999, Damon Jones approached P.J. Carlesimo's hotel room with cautious optimism. He knocked on the door and the Golden State Warriors coach opened it. He asked Jones to have a seat. Twenty-four hours earlier, the second-year guard had given Carlesimo a career game, collecting 17 points and five assists against the Utah Jazz. Jones was hoping that Carlesimo wanted to compliment him on his play. Instead the coach removed his glasses and turned his attention from the TV.

"There's no easy way for me to say this," Carlesimo said.

He did not have to finish. Jones had been down this road before. Signed by Orlando on January 21, 1999...waived twelve days later. Signed by New Jersey on February 15...waived March 8. Signed by Boston on April 14...waived May 5.

The next morning, Jones was on a plane home to Galveston, Texas, out of work again. Undrafted out of the University of Houston, he played for eight different NBA teams in six years before Miami gave him his current address.

"You start to ask yourself if they're all right about you," says Jones of the long list of coaches and GMs who passed on him. "But I never stopped believing I'd get to this point."

Jones hates the J word (journeyman). Don't dare use it around him. "To me that says you're not good enough, that you don't work hard enough. As soon as a reporter uses that word, the interview is over." He has absolutely no desire to revisit the past. "Let's talk about what I'm doing now," he says. "Look, I got one of the highest winning percentages of any starting point guard in the NBA. What does that tell you? That I'm valuable. So why all these teams keep trading me?"

What he lacks in skill, he makes up for with personality. His biting wit has made him one of the most popular players in the league. Minnesota's Sam Cassell calls on a regular basis to get his licks in. So does Portland's Nick Van Exel. And Orlando's Cuttino Mobley. And Boston's Paul Pierce. And Orlando's Steve Francis.

Jones gets gridiron love, too. "Hang with him for just a little while and you can see he's one of the funniest guys around," says wide receiver Terrell Owens of the National Football League.

The point guard's standup routine has transformed the Heat locker room, but his leadership role is no joke. After he cracked Miami's starting lineup on December 6, the team went on a 16–1 run. Why? Because Jones is not shy about getting in Dwyane Wade's ear or pointing Shaq in the right direction. In fact, the big man appears to genuinely love the prodding. The ice on Jone's wrist, neck, and watch? Gifts from Shaq. When Jones' sneaker deal fell through, Shaq got him another one—to rock his signature shoe.

"He's my best friend," says Jones. "I'm funnier, more handsome and dress better but he's still my boy." The two are so tight, teammates playfully refer to Jones as Donkey to Shaq's Shrek. Jones laughs it off because he knows it comes from a good place—the heart of a team.

In August of 2002, in a pick-up game at Houston's Westside Tennis Club starring Steve Francis, Rashard Lewis, and Robert Horry, the unemployed Jones ripped into former Rocket Dan Langhi for failing to display NBA-level intensity. "You gotta go hard all the time," he shouted. "You never know who's watching!" Now that Jones runs with the in-crowd, he's no less willing to share that hard-earned wisdom. Whenever the vets gather to eat dinner or watch a ballgame, Jones always remembers to include the rookies. "He kind of took me under his wing when I was in college," says teammate Rasual Butler. "He showed me how to carry myself on the court, in the club, wherever. He's always been supportive. Even when he wasn't in the league. "You're not going to find a teammate like D.J. anywhere."

And yet, I don't need a map to locate him before tonight's game. He's holding court at his locker, mouth running a mile a minute.

"Hey, U, you got my lotion?" he asks Udonis Haslem.

"Rasual, what you gonna do tonight, baby?"

The boys are loose when they take the court—all but guard Eddie Jones. With 0.4 seconds remaining, he misses a crucial free throw against the SuperSonics, snapping Miami's franchise-record winning streak at fourteen games. Hey, you can't win 'em all.

LOS ANGELES, JANUARY 10

THIS SUCKS! I'VE BEEN here for two days and I have yet to see the sun. A week and a half into 2005, Los Angeles has been hit with twenty-one inches of rain and there's no sign of the weather clearing up. It's 10:33 on a Monday night and I'm here in my hotel room typing away when I could be at Miyagi's mingling with Miss Nikki or some young thing with stars in her eyes fresh off the bus from Topeka.

LOS ANGELES, JANUARY 12

IT FINALLY STOPS RAINING and I celebrate by sleeping the day away. For some reason, my mental alarm clock doesn't work on the West Coast. It's 3:20 p.m. when I crawl out of bed and find precious sunlight creeping through the curtains. I feel like Howard Hughes.

After checking my e-mail for annoying directives from my editor about missing quotes or long-past deadlines—"Do you realize your story is due today?!" is always a good one—I pick up my trusty NBA Blue Book and peruse the schedule. The Blue Book is the reporter's bible. It contains the phone numbers of the media relations staff for all thirty teams as well as information on team hotels and restaurants, and directions to practice facilities. Just try and get through a season without one.

The Heat are in town in two days to play the Clippers. The game will mark Shaq's first trip to Los Angeles since his ultra-hyped Christmas Day clash with Kobe. It will also be a homecoming of sorts for point guard Keyon Dooling, who spent the first four years of his career in a Clippers uniform. I want to call him to set up a time to meet, but I can't seem to penetrate his cellular defense system. *A full mailbox?* I never heard of such a thing, not until I started hanging out with NBA types. *You can't leave a message. Sorry. Have a nice life.* Most players never actually answer their cell phones, so the only way to communicate with them is by leaving your number and growing old while you wait for them to call back. Often the gambit requires an in-person, follow-up conversation that goes something like this.

Me: Man, I tried to call you, but your mailbox was full.

Player: *For real?*

Elton Brand rings up 19 points and four blocks today, leading the Clippers to a 103–92 win over the Seattle SuperSonics, the best team in the NBA's Northwest Division. He's making a late run at the All-Star team, but don't expect to find him waiting by the phone. He won't be the least bit surprised if he's snubbed. When you don't play above the rim, you find yourself below the radar—beyond the purview of the fans who choose the starters. If Brand's going to make the cut, it'll be because of the coaches who fill out the roster. He can really use a win streak to support the cause right now, but the Clips rarely win back-to-back games, much less three or four in a row.

Oh, well. I myself am a lock for the All-Star game. I go every year for *The Magazine*. Worse comes to worse, I'll send him a postcard.

Frankie Muniz and his boys are camped on the Staples Center court waiting for the players to wrap up their interviews. Just as I'm about to enter the tunnel to the locker rooms, a voice calls out.

"Chris, hey, Chris, yo, it's me!"

Former Nicholls State power forward Chris Bacon is walking toward me with arms extended for some brotherly love. He's wearing a size fifty-four Rashard Lewis jersey. In 2001, I tried out for the National Basketball Developmental League for a story I was writing about the long, unforgiving road to the NBA. Bacon was one of the players I bonded with at the week long training camp.

"Oh, shit, what's up, man?" I ask.

"I'm here for my boy Rashard, man. You know I got to represent my people. What are you up to man? Shit, we ain't seen each other in forever."

"Still covering the league. Thought you would've gotten that call by now."

Damn, how Bacon wants that call. Realistically, there's little chance it will come. Sure he's Rashard's boy, but that doesn't mean he can box out Udonis Haslem or stop Shawn Marion on the break. He's an undrafted, 25-year-old forward coming off major knee surgery. Last year, eight NBA teams used their first-round picks on high school players.

He rolls up his pant leg and shows me a six-inch vertical scar. I'm no pessimist, but this is the reality of today's game. In the mid-Nineties, 25 meant you were a young player who took his lumps and learned from the older guys. Today, 25 means you are the older guy.

Bacon can't see this, though. Not with his head in the clouds. He drives big cars and stays at Lewis's cavernous house in suburban Seattle when the Sonics are on the road. When the players go out after a game, he's there too. Always the life of the party. He works out with NBA guys and has enough talent to play the crash test dummy during their summer pick-up games in Houston.

No matter what name you throw at him, he tells you he's tight with that person. "Kobe's my man," he brags. "He calls me Shakin' Bacon. I call him K Smooth. That's my dog. I mess with him all the time." Mention a happening gym, he played there last week. That new club? He already knows the bouncer. See those girls in the third row? Want to meet them? Bacon never lets on that he doesn't have the answer. Because guys without answers don't make the league.

"I'm working out now, getting everything back, you know?" he says. "Gotta have my shit prepared, man. Chris, you know me, I'm all about getting to the league. It's on my mind 24/7. When I wake up and when I go to sleep that's all I think about…All I need is the opportunity, then I'ma take it from there. It's gonna be on."

Bacon stops me in mid-step, leans in close and quietly asks, "You know any agents?"

Muniz and his boys are outside the lockerroom now, spying the Clippers Spirit Dancers as they trickle one by one out of a nearby door.

"Who...The brunette with the shoulder-length hair?" Muniz says. "Yeah, I know her." He's talking about the perky cheerleader I was eyeballing in November. He walks over and gives her a hug. Looks like Malcolm's all grown up. Even if the woman is two inches taller than him. Fame sure is sweet.

I leave them alone and head off in search of Brand. He sits at his corner locker with his size nineteen feet in a twenty-gallon tub of ice water. This is one of the more unpleasant aspects of being a professional athlete. If you think it's easy, try it sometime. Talk to me after, say, forty-five seconds. For most pro athletes, though, icing is no big deal. They've been doing it their whole careers. The one drawback: You're stuck at your locker in plain view of the press for at least twenty minutes.

"This is what we needed," Brand says, savoring tonight's win. "Players always talk about team confidence, but it's so true. We have to know we can beat teams when we walk onto the floor."

This is the point in the season when most Clippers teams begin their descent into mediocrity. But this bunch is different. They close out games when they have the fourth-quarter lead. They don't get rattled when they fall behind. That's what confidence does.

LOS ANGELES, JANUARY 13

DOOLING'S MAILBOX IS STILL full so I have nothing to do. Brand's "taking it easy tonight." Shaq's coming to town and the man's got to get his rest. A few years back, Brand and I stayed out late at Dublin's on Sunset Boulevard on the eve of a Clippers-Lakers game. All Brand could think about was putting a body on Shaq. He was stiff as a board. After two Jack & Cokes with agent David Falk shouting into my ear above the music about the luxury tax, I learned a valuable lesson. It's best to let Brand be.

Think I'll fly solo to the Staples Center for LeBron vs. Kobe. Kobe's been relishing this match-up. He wants to prove he's still the NBA's Alpha man. Last season, while he was defending himself against a sexual assault charge in Colorado, people were afraid to talk to him. Now that jail time is no longer an issue, everyone's lining up to get in their jabs. He's traded furious, often-childish, barbs with Shaq, accused Karl Malone of trying to make time with his wife, Vanessa, and served as a punching bag for every talk radio nitwit in America.

LeBron is the new M.J., a role Kobe eyed with envy for years. He's got that $90 million sneaker contract with Nike and a series of commercials in constant rotation. Kobe signed with Nike in the summer of 2003—for half LeBron's fee—after buying his way out of his contract with Adidas. (An Adidas staffer once told me that Kobe was enraged to discover an entire wall devoted to Tracy McGrady at the company's Santa Monica store.) But due to his legal problems, Kobe's Nike commercials never aired. His reign as the company's premier pitchman was over before it started. And now, his No. 8 Lakers jersey, once the league's best seller, has fallen from the NBA's top fifty. The new No. 1 belongs to Shaq's teammate Dwyane Wade. (In fact, his home, road, and alternate jerseys all rank in the top ten.) Throw in the fact that Kobe's Lakers are off to an 18–15 start and you see why he's hellbent on proving his worth.

With his ankles freshly wrapped in Lakers yellow tape, he walks from the trainer's room and sits at the locker to the left of Brian Cook, methodically slipping his feet into his purple, yellow, and white Nike Air Zoom Huarache 2K4s. Unlike LeBron, Kobe doesn't have his own signature shoe. When he stands up and bounces on the balls of his feet, I detect an extra spring in his step. Kobe loves challenges. Former Lakers coach Phil Jackson once accused him of sabotaging high school games just so he could bring the team back with a rousing, one-man show. This is, in part, why his feud with Shaq has dragged on for so long. To Kobe, the thrill of outwitting and outshooting such a massive force is irresistible. Now Jackson's gone and Shaq's gone—along with every other player from the Lakers' 2002 championship roster except Slava Medvedenko—and Kobe has to invent new challenges. Like, say, getting the best of LeBron and his red hot, Central Division-leading Cavaliers on national TV.

Out in the arena, the stars are in full force: Donald Trump, Ashton Kutcher, Chris Rock, and Andy Garcia. When I arrive at press row, longtime L.A. sportscaster Jim Hill is hobnobbing with Denzel Washington. To get to my seat, I literally have to put a body on the Oscar-winning actor, hooking him with my elbow much like a post player trying to turn the corner on the block.

Kobe misses a jumper on the Lakers' first possession. Minutes later, LeBron catches a pass from point guard Jeff McInnis on the left wing just beyond the three-point line. Kobe quickly presses up on him. LeBron turns his left side to Kobe and, still facing him, holds the ball away like a teenager playing a game of keep-away. This is a move invented by Michael Jordan. Born of his complete and sustained domination of the NBA, it's the ultimate sign of confidence. Whenever M.J. cornered a hapless defender, turned a cold shoulder to him, and extended the ball out behind his head in that giant right hand of his, he was saying, "I have absolute control of this game. While I ponder the many options I have to destroy you, you will stand there and wait for me to hand you your ass."

Scores of young players have taken to copying the move. When they try it, however, they often disrupt the flow of the game. As they live out their Jordan fantasies, teammates collide like circus clowns rubbernecking an overturned car. Kobe once had the audacity to do it against Jordan himself. But coming from a lifelong M.J. worshipper, he saw it as an homage, an opportunity to show the master what he'd learned. He finished that game in Chicago with 33 points. Were he less careful, the move might have been misconstrued as a slight greater than his infamous All-Star Game wave-off of Karl Malone.

Kobe executes Jordan's move flawlessly. But most young bucks try to do it when the shot clock is running down. Instead of ticking off their options, they watch them fly out the window, leaving themselves with an off-balance jumper. Allen Iverson's hands are too small to securely palm the ball, so he has to hold it down low with his palm facing up. Steve Francis has watched taller players swat the ball away. In his early years in Toronto, Vince Carter seemed to try the move on every other play, significantly curtailing its impact. Tracy McGrady, too.

But LeBron has given the move his own unique flair. Bending at the waist as if to catch his breath, he lowers the ball instead of raising it. The action isn't intended to emasculate his defender or to scream "Look at me!", but to buy him time to find the teammate with the best shot. On this night, he straightens up and zips a pass to Zydrunas Ilgauskas, who misses a chippy.

The dynamic duel ends right there. One Cavs possession later, with 5:39 remaining in the first quarter, Kobe leaps to grab a missed LeBron layup. As he returns to Earth, his right Nike Air Zoom, the one he wears in lieu of a signature shoe, comes down on the foot of Cavalier Ira Newble.

"Shiiiit!!!" Kobe screams. "Oh my God! Shit!" He collapses to the floor in a heap. The crowd as one holds its breath. Kobe is on his knees, his forehead smooshed flat on the Staples Center floor. He's gnashing his teeth. Pounding the court with his fist.

"Fuck!" he shouts, rolling onto his back and grimacing in pain, clutching at his severely-sprained right ankle. His wife, Vanessa, covers her mouth with her hands in the stands. Lakers trainer Gary Vitti rushes onto the court, kneeling down beside Kobe and putting his hand on his knee. He leans over in the way trainers do when they ask a downed player where it hurts. You can see the concern on his face. After five long minutes, Kobe is helped off the floor. He will not return. Life has left the building.

The Lakers win 98–94. LeBron finishes with 28 points. When the Lakers' boyish rookie guard Sasha Vujacic, drafted in June with the 27th pick, leaves the locker room, TV and newspaper reporters are still waiting for Kobe to emerge from the trainer's room. I scan the CDs in his locker, including two by artists I do not recognize: Paul Jackson, Jr., and Chris Botti. Botti's is titled *A Thousand Kisses Deep*.

At long last, Kobe steps from the trainer's room sporting a brown Nike sweatsuit that looks extremely comfortable and two crutches that do not. The bounce in his step is gone. He limps to his locker and sits down.

"This is the first injury I've suffered in the course of a game where it didn't cross my mind that I'd be back," he says in a voice that would make an undertaker sound cheery. After fielding a few more questions, he realizes that the press has detected his sudden vulnerability. He tries to leave on an upbeat note. "This is all about challenges," he says, firming up his voice. "That's what we've been doing all season long, responding to challenges. I think eventually this will make us better. It will be a positive thing for us, no doubt."

As I leave the room, I glance back. Kobe looks like a forlorn kid staring out the back of his parents' station wagon on the way to a new neighborhood. The Lakers are 19–15, sitting in the No. 10 spot in the Western Conference. His return to greatness will have to wait at least four more weeks.

In the bowels of the Staples Center minutes later, a voice calls out from behind me: "Step aside please! Coming through!" I turn to find one of those carts that whisk elderly people through airports. On the back sits Kobe, his bandaged leg hanging off the edge like a loaf of French bread in an overstuffed shopping cart. Vanessa sits next to him. Aluminum crutches separate the two.

Kobe looks up as the cart slows to pass. His hand is on Vanessa's leg. Her hand is on his.

"How do you feel, man?" I ask.

"Good. I feel good."

He thrusts out his hand for a shake. I reach out just as the cart picks up speed. Kobe leans forward as if to help me up off the court. Our fingertips graze. Vanessa laughs.

"Next time," Kobe says, a big smile on his face.

DETROIT, JANUARY 15

LIKE I SAID, WAITING is a big part of my job. But there's waiting and then there's waiting for Richard Hamilton. The Pistons' running joke is that when Rip's involved, Greenwich Mean Time goes out the window. Rip shows up whenever Rip feels like it. If he's supposed to be at a charity function at 5, feel blessed if he shows up at 5:30.

Meeting him for dinner at 8? Well, don't kill yourself to get there.

Don't misunderstand. Rip Time doesn't apply to practice, games, or team flights. He's often one of the first to arrive for basketball-related functions. He knows what pays the bills. But the rest of the time you, me, and everybody else has to adjust to his time zone.

Hamilton's such an easygoing guy, it's hard to get him, well, going. He may first want to run back another game of Madden football or round up his buddies and load them into the Range Rover. No sense trying to figure it out. Just roll with it.

I arrive in Detroit too late to catch the Sixers-Pistons game. It's my first DNP of the season. At about 10 o'clock, I give Josh Nochimson, who also happens to be Rip's business manager, a call. He tells me Rip had 25 points and six assists in the Pistons, 99–95 win. He doesn't know I saw the game on TV.

"I think everyone's about to get together," he says. "You want to hang out?"

"Yeah, what's the plan?"

"I'll give you a call in about an hour. Let me call Rip and try to put something together. If you don't hear from me, call me."

"Solid."

I can already imagine the excuses I'll hear tomorrow. An hour passes and, what a surprise, my cell doesn't ring. I leave Nochimson a message, telling him to call me in the morning. Then I order Domino's, watch Frankie Muniz tell Conan O'Brien he's too short to get chicks and go to sleep. It's hard to tell if I was a victim of Rip Time or not.

You have to understand that as a writer, no matter how close you think you are to an athlete, you're not a player. And if you're not a player, you can plan on watching a lot of TV. Whenever I make plans with Hamilton or Jones or Brand, whether to meet for lunch or some other activity outside the arena, I'm never certain it's going to happen until I'm in the car sitting right next to him. The more people swirling around an NBA star, the higher the odds your plans will fall through. They've got too many distractions. And, because they've got teams of handlers to perform every little chore for them, the act of getting into a car and driving to meet someone is a monumental task. It's much easier to hit the reset button on the PS2 and apologize the following day. On top of that, there's the Confusion Factor. Maybe it's unique to me, but when I'm coordinating plans with professional ballplayers, they seem to speak another language.

Brand and I once agreed to meet for lunch at Aunt Kizzy's Back Porch, a soul food joint not far from his old apartment in Marina del Rey. I hooked up with him in the parking lot outside the Clippers practice facility.

"I got something to do real quick," he said, "but just follow me and I'll meet you there later."

Now what the hell does that mean? Do I follow him or not? Before I could phrase the question, Brand was pulling out of the parking lot.

"Fuck it," I said and raced to my car.

On another occasion, back when Jamal Crawford was playing in Chicago, I arranged to meet him outside the team's practice facility and follow him to his house. "I drive a black Escalade with rims," he said before disappearing into the locker room. I sprinted to the player's parking lot and discovered six black Escalades with rims. Now, for reasons I've made abundantly clear, I could not call his cell phone to ask which one was his. I had to stake out the exit instead.

Because it was freezing outside and I feared frostbite, I ran to my rental car first. The moment I got behind the wheel, I saw a black Escalade flying by me in the rearview mirror. I had to decide right then and there if I was going to chase it. Lose Crawford and the day is done. I drove behind the Escalade for a good six miles before I noticed the Washington State license plates. Being that Crawford was the only Bull from that state, I felt relieved. And a little foolish.

DETROIT, JANUARY 17

THE MAYBACH GLIDES TO a halt in the parking lot outside the Palace of Auburn Hills and the doors fly open, dispensing Richard Hamilton's boys into the light. Hamilton himself steps from the passenger seat. His mink coat is unzipped, revealing one of his signature Rip City jerseys, a tribute to his hometown of Coatesville. Few passions in sports come close to Hamilton's devotion to his blue-collar birthplace forty-four miles west of Philly. "No one ever wants to gives us respect," he says. "There used to be a sign on the highway that let you know when you got to Coatesville, but they took it down. Then I looked on a map and we weren't even there. Where's the respect?"

Because the downtrodden steel town gave him life, because it kept him out of trouble, taught him values, and introduced him to basketball, he's made it a lifelong goal to put it back on the map. "Everything I have I owe to Coatesville," he says. "That's where my heart beats."

With the exception of the fifteen-minute drive to and from practice, Hamilton rarely goes anywhere by himself. Make that never. Not to the grocery store. Not to the West Indies. There are very few moments in his life that his childhood buddies have not witnessed.

"If I looked around and [my friends] weren't there, I wouldn't feel right," he says. "Once I drove to a game by myself and the parking attendant looked at me like something was wrong."

The guys followed him from Coatesville Area High to the University of Connecticut, where he led the Huskies to a 34–2 record and a national championship in 1999. They moved west with him to Detroit, where he won an NBA championship in 2004. With each lifestyle change, each new demand on his time, the guys were there to keep him grounded. Says cousin Jontue Long, "We'd be walking down the street and people would be pulling him in all different directions asking for pictures and autographs and we'd just be left standing there. At first it was awkward because we didn't really know how to act." But when the crowds dispersed, Rip's boys saw that he was just as puzzled as they were. "He was rich and famous but he was still Rip," says Long. "He was still Coatesville."

Still the same kid who'd sneak into darkened rooms at basketball camp with one hand full of lotion and another full of baby powder and smear them onto some poor kid's face. He'd wait till breakfast the next morning to see which one walked into the mess hall tarred and feathered, all the while cracking up.

"We're not his entourage or his posse," says Mark Brown, a financial advisor with Smith Barney, whose dark blue business suits stick out among the legion of Rip City jerseys. "Our friendship is from the heart, as real as anything there is. We all have our own productive lives, but we've been together forever."

To seal their bond and pledge their allegiance to Coatesville, ten members of Rip's crew have CV FOR LIFE tattooed on their abdomens. The 11th member declined to join them with good reason: "He has a big stomach, so we let him get it on his shoulder," says Rip. Hamilton has CV on his jewel-encrusted bling, on his license plates and etched into the back of his game shoes, too. For him, all things begin and end with the town where he was born.

With the season nearing the halfway point, though, Rip's Pistons have yet to find their groove. For a team with such talent, they have a mind-boggling propensity for overlooking the extra pass, standing around on offense, and barely striking iron with their jumpshots. But you won't find twelve players who know each other better. If Rasheed Wallace's corner three is falling, his teammates find a way to get him the ball. If Ben Wallace suddenly streaks downcourt, they know just where to hit him with the lob.

Against the Memphis Grizzlies a week and a half ago, however, none of that was evident. For the first time in history, an NBA player led his team in scoring without making a single shot from the field. All 14 of Hamilton's points came on free throws. He went 0-for-10 on the floor. "I never thought I'd have to coach effort," said Larry Brown. "I've never had to do that in my entire life, and this is the last group I expected to do it with."

ORLANDO, JANUARY 18

DOUG CHRISTIE SITS AT his locker, flipping through his newly-acquired Orlando Magic playbook. A week earlier, he was living in Sacramento, playing for the Kings. Now he's hustling to introduce himself to his teammates and rushing to memorize dozens of offensive sets. He's not surprised to be here, though: Defense is his specialty and Orlando's D is so spotty that general manager John Weisbrod eagerly parted with proven scorer Cuttino Mobley to shore it up, even though the trade angered Mobley's close friend Steve Francis, the team's point guard.

Christie's spirited play proves infectious. Hamilton doesn't have an off night per se, hitting 9 of 16 shots from the field (including 8 of 8 from the stripe), but thanks to Christie's relentless hounding, he works hard for those shots. Instead of chipping away at the Magic with his pet eighteen footer, Hamilton is forced to catch the ball out beyond the three-point arc, where he has to put it on the floor to get his desired shot. As a result, the Pistons offense plays a touch out of sync and the Magic notch nine steals (four compliments of you know who).

"It felt like one of those old-school high school situations where the coach puts a guy in the game to do nothing but shut a man down," Hamilton says. "Doug didn't help on anyone else all night. He just hounded me and denied me the ball every second he was on the court."

Christie did one other thing that Hamilton didn't expect: He drilled a clutch three with 1:26 remaining to give the Magic a 98–96 lead. They never trailed again, putting the champs away, 103–101. The game literally left the Pistons holding their noses. At halftime, the Magic's youth foundation presented Canine Companions for Independence with a $10,000 check. The seeing-eye dog that accompanied the group onto the floor relieved itself on the hardwood right under the Detroit basket. When the Pistons came out to warm up, they steadfastly avoided the doggie waste.

"Did they tell you what was on the floor," I ask Rip.

"I heard it was dog shit. Was it?"

"You heard right."

"Man, I've never heard of anything like that. Like I said, just one of those crazy nights."

ORLANDO, JANUARY 20

IT'S ALWAYS INTERESTING TO see a player return to play in the place he once called home. For a player of T-Mac's caliber, it's a major news event. Shortly after 11 o'clock in the morning, he leaves his locker in the TD Waterhouse Centre to address the Orlando media. Thirty-five members of the press are camped outside the door. Their mood is decidedly ornery. As journalists tend to do when a story makes them wait, they've grown more and more antsy with each passing minute. One guy sighs. Another fiddles with his microphone. And, as if on cue, two of them start a mundane debate about batting average or field goal percentage.

When McGrady finally steps into view, he gives me a playful jab to the ribs, followed by a pound. In that casual way of his, he asks me how things are going while the ugly horde waits with cameras and baited breath to ask him what it's like to be back in the place that unceremoniously traded him to Houston. The moment he turns to the mob, the bright camera lights flash in his eyes and the tape recorders come rushing toward his chin.

Unlike most of his peers, T-Mac loves fielding questions from the media. He views it as a game. Because he sounds so frank in his sound bites, you might think he speaks without thinking. But nothing could be further from the truth. What you don't see on the 11 o'clock news are the long pauses, the *hmmmms* and the head scratches. "That's a tough question," he will say while pursing his lips to buy time to put his thoughts in order.

He's an artisan of the Q&A session, a member in good standing of the league's all-interview team. But this wasn't always so. After being selected with the ninth pick in the 1997 draft, the third player in two years to jump from high school to the pros, the 18-year-old

McGrady found himself in Toronto struggling to adjust to the NBA and having to field questions from prying reporters. He had yet to find his role in the Raptors' offense and the arctic Canadian winter had blindsided him. The NBA was supposed to be glamorous, he thought. This wasn't. Raptors head coach Darrell Walker only made matters worse. Not only did he withhold playing time from his young prodigy, he rode him unmercifully in practice. He mistook McGrady's sleepy demeanor for loafing.

"I used to kill those guys in practice," T-Mac insists. "Everybody knew Darrell Walker didn't like me."

He was so depressed that he'd sleep day and night. A shy kid, he didn't have much in common with his older teammates. Guys like Marcus Camby and Damon Stoudamire were cool, but they couldn't help him shake his disappointment. When reporters approached him, usually to ask if he had any regrets about skipping college, McGrady's shaky voice was barely audible. He looked down when he spoke, avoided eye contact, and let his sentences trail off. One of the few escapes he had was calling home. More often than not, the voice on the other end of the phone belonged to his girlfriend, Clarenda Harris.

After his senior season at Mount Zion Christian Academy in North Carolina, McGrady had signed a five-year, $12-million shoe contract with Adidas and then strolled into the Lexus dealership where Harris worked. She impressed him much more than the SC 400 coupe, so he left with her phone number.

Harris wasn't into basketball players. She'd heard too many stories about posses and groupies and endless road trips. At 22, she wasn't looking for a boyfriend four years her junior. But McGrady was persistent. He called her and called her until she agreed to go out with him. On their first date, he took her to a sports bar where they ate chicken fingers and watched the Bulls and the Jazz in the NBA Finals. When McGrady moved up north for his rookie season, he rang up great big roaming charges. "It was pretty crazy," he says. "I'd get a phone bill and it would be like a thousand dollars."

Harris knew there was more to McGrady than a quiet side. She also knew he'd have to reveal it if he was going to be as successful as he promised. She began to coach him in public speaking, teaching him to project his voice and look interviewers in the eye. She hired an image consultant and McGrady's confidence grew.

By his second season in the league, he was looking forward to post-game interviews. His cousin, the dynamic Vince Carter, had arrived in Toronto to lure him out of his shell, and his comfort in front of the TV cameras and willingness to speak his mind soon made him a local media favorite.

When he leans up against the white concrete wall outside the lock-erroom in the TD Waterhouse Centre six years later, the press is expecting something big. McGrady wants to shine, but he has to be careful. This isn't softball practice. He knows what to expect. To many of the fans who cheered him in this arena, he's dead.

"Any harsh feelings toward the Magic for the way things came to an end?" asks a beat writer.

McGrady puts his hands behind his back. A wry smile crosses his lips. Rockets media relations director Nelson Luis stands to his right. He's got a worried look on his face.

"Not at all," replies McGrady with a chuckle. "That was the past. You guys don't expect me to think about that forever, do you?"

"But does it give you extra incentive?"

"Of course, I want to destroy them. Any time someone tells you they don't want you around, you want to make them pay. I wish it could have ended on a better note, but sometimes things happen like that. I definitely regret some of the things I said and the way I felt, but it happened and there's nothing I can do about it now."

He has an answer for everything. After a dozen or so revenge-related questions, a TV reporter with a dark blue suit and slicked-back hair forces his way to the front of the pack and sticks his microphone in McGrady's face.

"Can you talk about the lawsuit," he chirps. "Will it be settled? Do you feel bad? What can you tell us about the lawsuit?"

The group's ears suddenly prick up. This is an unexpected curve-ball.

"I feel terrible about it, just awful," replies McGrady, down-shifting his mood to somber. A 57-year-old maintenance man named Fred Chamberlin who worked at McGrady's Orlando mansion has just filed a lawsuit in Orange County Circuit Court seeking unspecified damages. According to Chamberlin's attorney, Eric Faddis, the plaintiff was climbing the stairs to the second floor of T-Mac's home when McGrady's rottweiler, Mac, lunged at him, causing him to topple backward. The dog clamped his powerful jaw on Chamberlin's face, says Faddis, tearing off the tip of his nose. Chamberlin had reconstructive surgery following the August 2004 attack, but Faddis says he'll have to go under the knife again.

"It was my dog and it damn near bit somebody's nose off," says McGrady. "He's a vicious dog, but I didn't think he had it in him."

The reporter peppers McGrady with a half dozen more questions. "What is this, Animal Planet?" an annoyed newspaper writer quips. McGrady handles the queries with his usual nonchalance, but Luis grows restless with each query.

"Are you going to have the dog put down?" asks the reporter.

"Are there any more basketball questions?" Luis interjects. "If not, we can wrap this up."

The cameras click off and the mob disperses. McGrady is left to wonder why things had to end so badly. Much like his Magic career.

HOURS LATER, HE STEPS off the elevator with Dikembe Mutombo in tow like some lanky, slow-moving bodyguard. As Tracy McGrady makes his way through the lobby of the Westin Grand Bohemian, minutes from the arena in downtown Orlando, he doesn't see TNT's Craig Sager hassling the concierge or the $220,000 silver Bentley coupe with the "Rent Me" sign parked in the driveway. On the verge of the biggest regular-season game of his eight-year career, he can barely keep his sleepy eyes open.

He's scheduled to play the villain in tonight's match-up. But right now, sleep sounds like a much better idea than sticking it to the Magic.

Moments before the game, his Rockets teammates gather outside the locker room waiting to be summoned into the arena. McGrady stands slightly apart from them. "It's time," someone shouts. They charge in unison out onto the court. For the next two hours, each time he touches the ball, McGrady will be met with a punishing chorus of boos. Fans hold signs denouncing their once favorite son. NO ME-MAC IN OUR TOWN, JUST ONE HILL OF A FRANCHISE and ORLANDO HATES ME-MAC, and, of course, T-MAC NEVER TRIES and HOUSTON WE HAVE A PROBLEM and WHEN THE GOING GETS TOUGH—QUIT.

When his name is announced over the P.A. system, McGrady claps for himself as jeers choke the air. He looks lonely, but his teammates understand the urgency of this game. They're not about to let him walk out of here with a loss.

Yao Ming and Steve Francis meet on the floor in a hug. They haven't seen each other since Francis left town in the McGrady trade.

After three years in the league, Yao is still stunned by the notion of dealing a player. Francis was good to him when he played in Houston, making sure that Yao never missed a weight-lifting session and treating him like one of the fellas. Seeing his old teammate in an Orlando uniform is troubling. Francis tells him not to worry—they'll always be friends.

After the tip, tempers rise like the mercury in mid-summer Mexico City. When McGrady touches the ball, he shows the crowd how little their noise bothers him by passing it to his teammates and letting the action come to him. He can't play it cool forever, though. Tonight is all about him. When he settles into his game, it's like old times. His pull-up from twenty feet out, the one he likes to set up with two hard left-handed dribbles, is ripping the cords. Even the boo mongers gasp when he swoops down the left baseline for a thunderous dunk.

McGrady often warns opposing fans that he plays better when they ride him. In his seven trips to Toronto, he's averaged 28 points. By halftime in Orlando, he has 12. His Rockets teammates are banging bodies and boards, giving Houston a 56–48 edge.

The play in the second half is even more physical. Francis, who also has something to prove, must be pulled away from nasty confrontations with Jon Barry and Bob Sura. "I led the league in technical fouls last season," he says. "If a guy is going to get in my face, I'm not a punk. I'm not a sucker, I just play hard."

McGrady does not back down either. Despite a furious, late-game comeback by Francis and Orlando, he spots up and slashes his way to 27 points, giving Houston a 108–99 victory. He does it without so much as cupping a hand to his ear.

During his post-game interview with Sager, hundreds of fans crowd the exit to the tunnel to pelt him with venom. The atmosphere is every bit as volatile as the one that sparked The Palace brawl in

November, but the Orlando fans are content to rattle McGrady's nerves. When he passes beneath them, he defiantly flexes his muscles, slowly nodding his head. In the stands above him, an ally unfurls a Rockets jersey and shouts, "I still love you, Tracy." McGrady's eyes light up. He points to the fan. For the first time all evening, he cracks a smile. The fan waves his red jersey like a bullfighter. McGrady pounds his chest, lowering his head and holding his right hand high. He extends his index finger skyward.

Minutes later, I enter the locker room to find a phalanx of reporters squeezed into a tiny corner in front of the chalkboard Jeff Van Gundy used to diagram plays at halftime. In the trainer's room nearby, McGrady's putting on his street clothes. League rules state that locker rooms must be open to the press no more than ten minutes after a game. Theoretically, this gives players time to settle their emotions without jeopardizing the media's deadlines. But NBA coaches almost always usurp that ten minutes, sending the players off to the showers in their towels just as the press files in. The bigger the star you are, the less likely that you can duck the prying eyes. And so, in the tradition of Michael Jordan, guys like Kobe Bryant, Kevin Garnett, Allen Iverson, and Vince Carter retreat to the trainer's room to dress. LeBron James must not be aware of the privileges of superstardom—perhaps he prefers to remain one of the fellas—but he has yet to seek this momentary refuge from the post-game frenzy.

The rabble-rousers are once again restless. Each time the door to the trainer's room opens, they snap up their tape recorders. When Charlie Ward steps into the light, they practically groan.

"Who y'all waiting for," he asks.

"We're waiting for you, man," I tell him.

A puzzled look crosses his face. He shakes his head and keeps on walking. "Tracy McGrady has left the building," he says.

After twenty long minutes, T-Mac emerges, dressed in a red and white striped Sean John shirt and an Adidas baseball cap.

"Look at you all pretty for the media," says Rockets trainer Keith Jones.

"All I wanted to do was win," McGrady proclaims. "The booing didn't bother me. It was to be expected. You guys wanted to make this a T-Mac versus Orlando thing, but it wasn't. It was Houston versus Orlando and we won."

A short time later, safely seated on the team bus, he stares out the window, viewing Orlando from a whole new perspective. He's tired yet again. Tired of playing the villain. The Rockets are bound for the airport and New York. Thirty minutes from now, he'll be fast asleep.

ORLANDO, JANUARY 21

IN THE MORNING'S *Orlando Sentinel*, the headline on the first sports page reads T-SMACKED in two-inch-high bold letters. Beneath it: T-Mac's Tally: 27 points, six rebounds, four assists. But Mike Bianchi can't resist taking one last parting shot, referring to McGrady as "T-Slack," "Me-Mac," and "McQuitter" in his column.

No matter. For McGrady, the road ahead looks a whole lot easier.

LOS ANGELES, JANUARY 26

LAKERS FORWARD LAMAR ODOM walks into the locker room and tosses a copy of the *Los Angeles Times* to the ground. Clipper guard Marko Jaric is talking junk, he announces, paraphrasing the guard from Serbia and Montenegro: "They play good basketball, but they aren't better than we are." Jaric's real quote is less inflammatory: "Obviously, they have a lot of talent; they play good basketball. But I still believe that we are a better team and we're going to show that sooner or later." But, coming from a player who averages 10 points and six assists—a player on a 19–22 team two spots removed from the playoffs—it's still a bold statement and the 22–17 Lakers aren't feeling especially conciliatory. All season long, they've been listening to the talk about their shortcomings, fielding wisecracks about how much they rely on Kobe Bryant to carry them. With Kobe on the sidelines nursing his ankle, Jaric's timing rings suspicious. "Him saying that is like a punter saying something," says Chucky Atkins. "I think that's pretty funny. We all were wondering why he wasn't saying that earlier in the season. Why's he saying it when we're without Kobe?"

Kobe himself had belittled the Clippers earlier in the season by saying that beating them was "old hat." He backed up that statement by leading the Lakers to wins in the teams' first two games. Tonight, in the third of their four meetings, the Clippers are going with a very straightforward game plan, says starting point guard Rick Brunson. "Just pound it in to Elton."

After shaking off nagging pains in his left knee and right index finger, Brand is beginning to round into form. He's notched a double double in each of his last seven games. On the Clipper's second possession of the evening, he begins his assault on number eight, taking a pass from Brunson, turning, and sinking a jumpshot. He adds nine more points to close out the half. He finishes with 28 points and 14 boards. The fired-up Clippers manhandle the Lakers in a 105–89 rout.

Head coach Mike Dunleavy cheerfully puts the outcome in perspective. "Of course it was a big game for us," he says. "I don't care that they didn't have Kobe. I don't care who they had. They could have put Rudy [Tomjanovich] out there and we were still going to try to win."

The Clips have ended a five-game slide with back-to-back wins. This is cause to celebrate.

LOS ANGELES, JANUARY 27

A LITTLE AFTER 10 in the morning, I wheel my rented Chevy Blazer through the ultra-slim streets high up in L.A.'s Hollywood Hills. My ears pop as I navigate the ribbon of road to the crib Elton Brand shares with his fiancé, Shahara Simmons. When I buzz the call box at the eight-foot-high, solid-oak gate, he answers it himself, dressed in a Clippers sweatsuit with a cell phone pressed to his ear.

"What up, C?" he says.

I give a polite nod so as not to interrupt his call and step lively along the front walk, which is nothing more than a koi pond—minus the fish—with square concrete platforms placed on top inches apart. Brand opens the front door and gives me the grand tour. We pass his massive DVD collection (more than 750 titles) and a big screen TV in the downstairs rec room. The ten-by-twenty-foot bed in the master bedroom could be a studio apartment in New York City. It's like nothing I've ever seen. "I just needed something a little bit bigger than normal," says Brand, quickly tossing a bra on a pile of laundry and sweeping aside a condom as if I haven't yet learned about the birds and the bees.

For the 25-year-old Clipper, this house is a symbol of personal and financial maturity. He bought it in the winter of 2003, not long after Los Angeles had secured his services for six more years to the tune of $80 million. Prior to that, he had lived alone in a one-bedroom, $2,700-a-month luxury high rise in Marina del Rey. No fewer than five of his Clipper teammates lived within earshot of him. With a 270 degree view of the water, it wasn't a bad place for a young bachelor to entertain. But Brand knew it was time to expand. L.A. was now his home, not some way station for underachieving lottery picks and passed-their-prime-vets. Simply talking about leading the Clippers to respectability wasn't good enough—he had to do it.

Step one was to set down some roots. And that meant wrenching his heart from Florida. In July of 2003, Pat Riley tried to lure him to Miami with an $80 million free agent offer. Brand was so elated—he loves Riley and South Beach—that he hopped a cross-country flight, walked the sand, and took a dip in the ocean. As he paddled away beneath the sun, he thought to himself, *This is it. This is how I want life to be.* After four lean years in Chicago and Los Angeles, he believed his career was about to take off. When he stepped from the ocean, there was a call waiting for him. The Clippers had matched. Just like that, Brand's vision of paradise disappeared in thin air. Two days later, he was back in L.A.

The tour of the house ends in the kitchen with a spectacular view of Los Angeles. Brand introduces me to his personal chef, Scott Wolf, who prepares us a breakfast of walnut pancakes, sausages, and orange juice. I didn't know Brand had a chef, but I'm not surprised. In the league, not having one is like not having an Escalade.

We sit down in a corner breakfast nook that reminds me of a booth at IHOP—if IHOP had a SoHo franchise. Brand tilts his thirty-two-inch, wall-mounted flatscreen toward us and casually surfs the channels. After a half dozen clicks, he comes to rest on a 50 Cent video for "Wanksta".

"The other day Corey [Maggette] rushed into the locker room and told everybody he heard 50 got his hand chopped off in his Lamborghini doors," he says, chuckling to himself.

He mutes the flatty and I ask him about Miami. He tugs on his Clipper sweats and eases back on the cushioned bench seats. "The week I was down there I was totally loving it," he says. "The thought of playing in Miami was unbelievable. But when the Clippers matched, I just kind of got over it. Was I disappointed? I mean, I've never been the type to complain. Shit, they're paying me $80 million dollars to be the man and play in sunny L.A. What's there to complain about? When they matched, I knew it was done. That's how the league works. If they match, it means they want you. That was it."

The video for Nelly and Tim McGraw's "Over and Over" comes on the silent TV.

"You like this song?" I ask.

"Not really. I mean it's all right. Something different."

He begins to channel surf again. Miami's still on his mind.

"When I got back to L.A., I made up my mind instantly that I was going to take this team places. I knew that's what I had to do. Miami was gone and I was upset, but the Clippers were still here. But you know what the funny thing is? If the Clippers hadn't matched, I'd have been the one playing for the Lakers this year, not Lamar Odom. Think about it. Miami would have traded me right back here for Shaq in a heartbeat. Either way, I was destined to be here."

Destined to be here. Not doomed to be here. Hey, they *are* paying him lots of cash.

MIAMI, JANUARY 30

WHAT A SCHEDULE! AFTER hanging out with Brand in L.A., I jump a jet to Miami for the highly-anticipated clash between the Heat and the Rockets. Playing to a packed house in front of a less-rabid crowd is a welcome treat for Tracy McGrady. Me? I'm psyched I get to watch the highlight duel between him and Dwyane Wade.

As I take my seat at the end of the first courtside media row, shuffling through the pre-game notes from the press room, Jay-Z sits in the pricey, celebrity seat next to me. I freeze. He's not only my favorite rapper, but a near god to the vast majority of players in the NBA. Ask any young baller who he'd rather have dinner with, M.J. or Jigga, and Jay wins almost every time. That's not why I tensed up though.

At the All-Star Game in L.A. last year, while the stagehands were prepping the Staples Center floor for Beyonce's halftime performance, I saw an opening and took it. The night before, I'd crashed the much-ballyhooed Players Association party, courtesy of Doug E. Fresh and his oversized entourage. I was standing on the sidewalk, secretly hatching a plan to smuggle myself inside, when his crew exited their limos and one of Fresh's boys looked up at me. I warmly extended my hand.

"What's up?" I said. "Chris from New York."

"What's up, player?" said Fresh's boy. A couple of fist pounds later, we were being whisked through the metal detectors and the party was on. A quick rule about attaching yourself to someone's crew: Once you get inside, get lost. It doesn't take long to figure you out and you'll end up like Kramer carrying around that Tony for Scarsdale Surprise. Or worse.

So naturally, when I saw Beyonce's boyfriend, Jay-Z, standing at the halfcourt sideline the following day, next to Denzel next to Ashton next to Chris Rock, I pulled down my New Era 59Fifty, cocked it to the side a bit, and parked myself a foot from the man's shoulder. *Sweet! Check me out! I'm a one-name superstar hanging on celebrity row!*

Jay-Z tapped my arm.

Oh shit. This is going to end one of two ways...

"You can't be here," he said.

"What?" I replied.

"They need this space right here so you can't stand there."

I got zero points for my Rocawear sweatshirt.

"My bad, man."

Now, here we are side by side again less than a year later and Jay-Z is looking my way. What are the odds he'll remember me?

Zilch.

Yet another meaningless nanosecond in the life of a celebrity. I mean, I was literally rubbing elbows...Well, what do you expect?

Jay-Z offers the slow-to-start McGrady a few words of encouragement. "Come on T-Mac! What's up, young boy! Let's go!" he shouts. The way I see it, that's the least he can do. When *The Blueprint* came out in 2001, McGrady bought six copies—one for each of his cars.

A few plays later, Udonis Haslem scoops up a loose ball in the lane. He's slow to go up with it, drawing the foul but watching his weak shot bound into the stands. Jay explains to the person sitting next to him how Haslem should have cocked the ball back. Just like they do it in Brooklyn's Marcy Projects.

During the first timeout, he summons his elephantine bodyguard, Sampson, and pulls out a large wad of cash—mostly twenties covered by a hundred-dollar bill. He peels off a dub and Sampson heads up the stairs to the concession stand. Beyonce's "Crazy In Love" blares over the P.A. system. Her boyfriend barely notices. Sampson returns with two medium Pepsis, two waters, a large popcorn, and no change.

With a minute and thirty seconds left in the half, Dwyane Wade blows by a Rockets defender with a spectacular crossover that brings

Jay-Z out of his seat. When D-Wade misses an acrobatic lay-up, the rapper clutches his fists to his head. Kind of like Stan Van Gundy.

The Heat are up 48–46 at the break.

Like so many NBA games, this one falls prey to that ugly third-quarter malaise. The fans are still returning to their seats a full five minutes in to the second half. Jay-Z is no different. At 7:57, he takes the stage once again and delivers a much more lively performance. Wade swoops to the hole and draws a foul. "Work that shit out," yells Jay. He offers up a "damn" on a T-Mac power move and converses with Shaq about something I can't quite make out. In the end, though, the young mogul can't go the full forty-eight. With two minutes remaining, he starts to yawn. Sampson leads the charge to the exit.

The Heat win 104–95. A middle-aged woman scrambles over to Jay-Z's seat to swipe the ticket stub he left behind. He didn't even touch his water. I find myself wondering how much I might get for it on eBay. Then I remember: I'm not a loser.

EASTERN CONFERENCE

ATLANTIC DIVISION

	W	L	PCT	GB	HOME	ROAD	LAST−10	STREAK
Philadelphia	21	23	.477	−	11−7	10−16	6−4	Won 2
Boston	21	24	.467	0.5	14−8	7−16	5−5	Lost 1
New Jersey	18	26	.409	3	9−9	9−17	6−4	Won 3
New York	18	26	.409	3	12−11	6−15	1−9	Lost 2
Toronto	18	27	.400	3.5	15−7	3−20	5−5	Lost 3

CENTRAL DIVISION

	W	L	PCT	GB	HOME	ROAD	LAST−10	STREAK
Cleveland	26	17	.605	−	16−4	10−13	5−5	Won 1
Detroit	26	18	.591	0.5	15−7	11−11	6−4	Won 3
Chicago	22	20	.524	3.5	15−10	7−10	8−2	Lost 1
Indiana	20	23	.465	6	10−10	10−13	3−7	Lost 5
Milwaukee	15	27	.357	10.5	10−10	5−17	3−7	Lost 3

SOUTHEAST DIVISION

	W	L	PCT	GB	HOME	ROAD	LAST−10	STREAK
Miami	33	13	.717	−	17−5	16−8	6−4	Won 3
Washington	26	17	.605	5.5	16−6	10−11	6−4	Lost 2
Orlando	24	20	.545	8	15−5	9−15	5−5	Lost 1
Charlotte	9	32	.220	21.5	8−13	1−19	1−9	Lost 1
Atlanta	9	34	.209	22.5	7−17	2−17	3−7	Won 1

WESTERN CONFERENCE

SOUTHWEST DIVISION

	W	L	PCT	GB	HOME	ROAD	LAST−10	STREAK
San Antonio	37	10	.787	−	23−1	14−9	8−2	Won 3
Dallas	28	14	.667	6.5	16−8	12−6	6−4	Lost 1
Memphis	26	20	.565	10.5	15−8	11−12	8−2	Won 2
Houston	25	21	.543	11.5	14−10	11−11	6−4	Won 1
New Orleans	8	36	.182	27.5	6−14	2−22	4−6	Lost 2

NORTHWEST DIVISION

	W	L	PCT	GB	HOME	ROAD	LAST−10	STREAK
Seattle	30	13	.698	−	16−6	14−7	5−5	Lost 1
Minnesota	24	20	.545	6.5	13−9	11−11	7−3	Lost 1
Denver	19	25	.432	11.5	12−9	7−16	5−5	Won 2
Portland	17	25	.405	12.5	10−9	7−16	3−7	Won 1
Utah	15	30	.333	16	9−12	6−18	4−6	Lost 2

PACIFIC DIVISION

	W	L	PCT	GB	HOME	ROAD	LAST−10	STREAK
Phoenix	36	10	.783	−	17−4	19−6	5−5	Won 5
Sacramento	30	13	.698	4.5	18−5	12−8	8−2	Won 2
L.A. Lakers	23	19	.548	11	16−9	7−10	5−5	Won 1
L.A. Clippers	22	23	.489	13.5	17−10	5−13	4−6	Won 2
Golden State	12	32	.273	23	9−14	3−18	1−9	Lost 5

THINGS TO SAY IN DENVER WHEN YOU'RE SLIGHTLY DRUNK

MIAMI, FEBRUARY 3

I LIKE TO STAY at the Biscayne Bay Marriott when I'm in Miami. It's only a mile from AmericanAirlines Arena and that's walking distance for me, even if it's blazing hot outside. My colleagues think I'm crazy—the ones with the forty-four-inch waists. I don't have the heart to tell them I do it so I'll never have a forty-four-inch waist.

There's nothing like walking to an NBA game. The closer you get, the more energetic you feel. Maybe it has something to do with the sea of red shirts crossing Biscayne Boulevard. Maybe it's the salsa pumping from the radio station van parked on the sidewalk. Who knows? I barely notice that my shirt is soaked with perspiration. My blood is pumping.

Five years ago, inside this very arena, former *Slam* writer Scoop Jackson, now with ESPN.com, advised me to reign in my excitement. "Get it out of your system," he said. I was a young reporter, bursting with adrenaline because I was about to see a playoff game between New York and Miami. It didn't matter that neither team had cracked sixty wins. I was going to watch some basketball. I feel the same way about Cleveland-Miami tonight. I can't wait to watch LeBron James on the break.

With 33 wins and 14 losses, Miami is the best team in the Eastern Conference. The 26–18 Cavs are neck and neck with the Pistons at the top of the Central Division. "Yeah, we have a better record, but there's still a chance for us to prove ourselves," says Heat coach Stan Van Gundy. This is a not-so-subtle reminder to his players that opponents with deep benches have lured Shaq into foul trouble.

Van Gundy's admonition is clearly justified. Sixteen seconds into the game, Zydrunas Ilgauskas pump fakes on the baseline, drawing a slap from Shaq. The Lithuanian center scores 11 points in the first five minutes. Everyone else on the court struggles to harness their excitement. Poor Damon Jones can't even attempt a shot, not with Jeff McInnis hounding him. Jones tries to rub the defender off with a baseline pick. McInnis grabs a handful of jersey. "He's holding me, dammit!" Jones screams at referee Jim Clark. Clark ignores him. Jones screeches to a halt at the next whistle, puts his hands on his hip, stares at the official incredulously.

Early in the second quarter, Van Gundy pulls Jones for Keyon Dooling, who ignites the Heat offense with 10 points in seven and a half minutes. We got ourselves a game.

As if cued to the rise in tempo, Oakland Raiders defensive tackle Warren Sapp and a Roc-A-fella Records executive make their entrance—fashionably late—taking the seats occupied by Jay-Z days earlier. The duo sets to work antagonizing everyone in uniform. Sapp, who has been making the rounds at NBA games recently, fancies himself a crude, potbellied Spike Lee. He's pals with a lot of league players—guys like Quentin Richardson, Eddie Jones, Ray Allen—many of whom he met via his good friend Michael Jordan.

To be a courtside celebrity is to be conflicted. On one hand, you want to soak up the applause when your image appears larger-than-life on the Jumbotron. But then you expose yourself to the public's cameras and pens. What to do? Well, if you're the lovely ladies of Destiny's Child, you take a seat at the TV table, next to TNT announcers Kevin Harlan and Doug Collins, smiling and waving at the camera, while the 300-pound bodyguard posting up behind you scares the commonfolk off with his don't-even-think-about-it glare. Hip-hop producer Pharrell, seated a few yards down the sideline in a diamond-studded sweatshirt with the words BILLIONAIRE BOYS CLUB emblazoned on the front and a red Chicago Bulls cap pulled tight on his head, simply tiptoes past the gawkers with his head down and shoulders hucked up as if he's running to the car in the rain. This tactic is a favorite of Hollywood celebrities like Ashton Kutcher, Leonardo DiCaprio, and Tobey Maguire. They seem to think it makes them invisible.

Warren Sapp must love to be seen. The 300-pound busybody can't stop fidgeting. The moment he settles into his seat, he notices the gaudy, walnut-sized championship ring on the right hand of Detroit Pistons scout George David, who's sitting courtside in press row. During a timeout, Sapp gets up and walks to Smith's side, proceeding to finger Smith's ring. The scout, who is talking on his cell phone and has never met Sapp, shifts the phone from his left hand to his right, giving the All Pro defensive tackle the slip. Sapp returns to his seat tail between his legs. In no time, though, he's back to talking junk with everyone within range. Dwyane Wade drives the lane, picking up a foul, and Sapps screams at referee Clark. "Hey, No. 6, I didn't come here to see a free throw shooting contest. These seats cost too much." Then Jones goes to the line and Sapp shifts his focus onto him. "D.J., you ain't doing nothing. Let me see something. You haven't even scored yet."

"It ain't about points," Jones shoots back. "Anyone can score."

"You can't."

"I'm only the starting point guard on the best team in the East. What do you want?"

I—like everyone else—am thinking I want to see LeBron do something. And, as if by magic, Damon feeds Eddie Jones on the wing and LeBron pounces, swatting up at the ball instead of down, knocking it out of Eddie's hands. LeBron corrals the loose ball and, with his head up, eyes scanning, ignites the break. Damon backpedals like mad, refusing to give up an easy bucket. He's alone at the foul line with LeBron closing fast. His options are dwindling. Damon steps back. He jumps. LeBron is in the air, rising and rising, gripping the ball like a grapefruit in his right hand and cocking it over his right shoulder. Damon has made a colossal mistake—a historic mistake. They tape these games in the NBA.

When their bodies collide, Damon doesn't put his arms out to block the shot. His body curls into a ball. He knows what's going to happen. Wishes like hell he had never jumped. He turns his body sideways, looking for cover. His right shoulder blade is tucked in LeBron's abdomen, his head buried in LeBron's armpit. LeBron uses his left hand to shove Damon out of the way. His right hand is still clutching the ball. He's still rising.

LeBron throws down a monstrous dunk. The building explodes. Damon crashes to Earth.

King James stops to scowl. Van Gundy calls time out. Shaq's eyes are as wide as saucers. The TNT cameras zoom in on LeBron's young face as he walks to the bench. The scowl fades, replaced by a smirk. At halfcourt, he's beaming so wide you can count his teeth.

Damon Jones walks to his bench without looking up. He can already hear the TNT anchors making fun of him. And his teammates and opponents and assistant coaches and friends. And Warren Sapp. That's the risk you take when you jump.

In the locker room after the game, LeBron sits in his shorts with his feet propped up on a metal folding chair, the kind professional wrestlers use to club each other with. Ice bags are taped to each of his knees. His jersey is crumpled on the floor inside-out. He picks through a Styrofoam container of chicken wings and a side of steamed vegetables. There's a Lipton Iced Tea at his side with the cap off, one sip shy of full.

"Man, my feet hurt," he says matter-of-factly. The Cleveland media is outside talking to his coach, Paul Silas, about the 100–88 loss. I ask LeBron about the dunk.

"Aw, it was nothing personal," he says. "I would have done that to anybody. Damon is a really good friend of mine so I had to get him. You know, it's just part of basketball."

Time to get Jones' point of view. I turn to go.

"Hey," LeBron calls out. I stop. "Tell Damon I'm sorry."

I had planned to hit the town with D.J., knock back a few drinks in some sweet South Beach night spot, but he's pulled a disappearing act so it's back to the hotel for me. As a card-carrying member of Procrasti-Nation, I'd like to postpone tonight's workload. Unfortunately, it's Thursday and everyone I know in Miami has to get up for work in the morning. Opening my laptop, I flick on the TV under the pretense of catching the second half of TNT's doubleheader: the Lakers versus the Spurs. Really I just want to hear what Ernie, Kenny, and Charles have to say about LeBron's big throwdown.

"Look out below Damon Jones! LeBron is bringing it on your head!" shouts Kenny Smith.

"Be on the lookout for the newest poster coming to a store near you," chimes in Charles Barkley.

The network replays the highlight eight times from four different angles and pauses the tape to examine Jones' facial expression. You can hear the crew laughing in the background. Just about every player in the league watches *Inside the NBA on TNT.* Some tune in for the highlights. Most want to see whom Kenny and Charles are clowning that night. Because the two of them played in the NBA and because they're not afraid to express their opinions, they get lots of respect. So do ESPN's Greg Anthony and Tim Legler. But hotshot anchors who try to hip up the highlights with outdated lingo don't impress.

"I have an official new nickname for Damon Jones," Kenny says. "You will now be known as Highlight, because that was the highlight of the year. Damon Jones a.k.a. Highlight coming to an arena near you."

Before I go to sleep, I try to reach Elton Brand on his cell phone. The Clippers started a back-breaking cross-country road swing tonight, nine games in twenty-one days, and I want to know what he's thinking. With Corey Maggette out of the lineup, the team beat the Grizzlies 106–103 to nudge its record to 23–23. I give Brand a half hour to call back and then it's lights out. I need some aspirin. There's a slight pain in one of my molars, lower jaw, right side. Oh, well, it's probably nothing.

MIAMI, FEBRUARY 5

WHEN I GOT THIS gig in November, I started a list of what ifs. What if I forget my tape recorder? What if so-and-so stands me up? What if a hurricane hits Miami when I'm there? Stuff like that. I also put together a list of things to avoid at all costs. I can not get arrested. I can not crash my hard drive. I can not have a dental emergency. When I woke up this morning, I scratched No. 3 off the list. The pain in my molar has been upgraded to a jolting current, kind of like having jumper cables connected to my choppers.

Oh, this is bad. Very bad.

MIAMI, FEBRUARY 6

I PRY MY LEFT eye open wide enough to see that it's 6:02 in the morning. Super Bowl Sunday. Before going to sleep last night, I pulled the cushions off the loveseat and wedged them into the gap in the curtains to block out all sunlight. This worked great except for the single sunbeam poking through the top of the curtain to hit me in the face. I have but one thought: *Today will not be a good day*. I need a dentist. Right now. Not tomorrow. Not the end of the week. Now. I'm freaking dying.

I'm supposed to meet Jones for lunch after practice. Not any more. I sit up. Lie down. Rinse my mouth with warm salty water. Nothing relieves the pain. I bang my head against the wall in frustration. Now I have a headache, too.

I walk to the gift shop in the lobby in my bare feet, wearing a pair of Knicks practice shorts I swiped from Allan Houston's locker at the 2001 All-Star Game. (When I saw Allen Iverson give Stephon Marbury a peck on the neck for hitting a key three late in the East's win, I knew then and there that Allan Houston had made his last All-Star appearance so I decided to borrow a souvenir.)

I want to buy some aspirin. The shop is closed. The elevator takes a year to climb back to the 18th floor. At the door to my room, I realize I don't have my key. I go back to the front desk to get a new one. I don't have any I.D. Fortunately, they know me here. Better still, the girl I have a crush on is off today. I'm not exactly looking my best.

Back in the room, I pace back and forth, taking long, deep breaths. I sit on the edge of the bed and rock back and forth while clutching a pillow. I lie down for four hours, then get up to log on to the Internet. I need to find a dentist. I haven't yet selected one in my insurance plan. Of course, if I had, chances are good that his office would be in Manhattan.

When I get to the insurer's homepage, I'm instructed to enter my username and password. Both are at my desk—in New York. I'm cooked. I slam shut my laptop and lie in bed for two more hours. Why is my whole life controlled by usernames and passwords?

At 1 o'clock, I remove the ice bag tied to my face with a T-shirt I ripped in half. I open the shades, get dressed, and head for my car. Maybe I can salvage the day. Fifteen minutes later, I'm standing outside the gym on the second floor of AmericanAirlines Arena with Miami's beat writers. One of them is telling me about the palm tree in his front yard.

Heat flack Tim Donovan swings open the door. "They're ready for viewing," he says.

What are we, at a wake?

The players are paired up, shooting their post-practice free throws. Under Coach Van Gundy's orders, they can't leave until their partner hits ten straight. Jones' partner? Shaq, of course. The game's most notorious free-throw shooter.

I join the media huddle in front of Van Gundy and stare holes in his forehead. I keep thinking about the searing pain that's going to shoot through my tooth the moment I ask him a question. I'm either going to scream or faint and fall to the ground with drool cascading down my lip. I feel like Gary McLain, the Villanova player who wrestled with visions of smacking President Reagan upside the head during the Wildcats post-championship visit to the White House in 1985.

I force out my question, get a blah-blah answer, and beat a quick retreat. Jones is heading for the locker room.

"Yo, D.J.," I call out. "What's up with this afternoon?"

Keyon Dooling has informed me that Jones is in a sour mood.

You might think it's the dunk that's bothering him. Distant memory. There are bigger things on his mind. Tina Thompson of the WNBA's Houston Comets has announced through the team that she's pregnant with Jones' baby and will be missing the start of the upcoming season. Jones has declined to talk to reporters about it. But clearly, he's distracted by the revelation. He's mired in his first real slump of the season. Dooling, his backup, is getting more and more playing time. That combination alone is enough reason for a player to blow off a writer.

"What's up, fam?" Jones says as he pulls open the door to the locker room. "Gimme fifteen minutes and meet me by the garage entrance."

Thirty-five minutes later, I'm sitting in my Buick Regal at the entrance to the player's parking garage, admiring sunny Biscayne Bay, one of those picturesque settings that television crews always use to establish the game-time atmosphere. Weatherbeaten *NBA on NBC* logos from the mid-Nineties, when the peacock owned the rights to broadcast league games, adorn the nearby concrete barriers. Who can forget the Knicks-Bulls clashes when M.J. was M.J. and Pat Riley roamed the New York sideline? Patrick Ewing's jump shot seemed to get better and better the lower Scottie Pippen's high top fade got. NBC started Marv Albert, Mike Fratello, and Ahmad Rashad. I used to dream about being an NBA reporter. Wondered what it would be like to ask those questions after the game. Maybe one of the players would inquire about my family. We'd make plans for dinner and I'd get an inside scoop and tell my friends how great it is to be in the league.

I start to hum the *NBA on NBC* theme music. A silver BMW 760i pulls out of the garage and slows as it passes me. The passenger window is down. Pat Riley eyes me suspiciously as he turns the wheel to the left to make the U-turn out of the garage. His front bumper comes dangerously close to one of those white concrete barriers.

Moments later, Jones pulls out of the garage in his silver 2005 Bentley coupe and taps the horn without stopping. I fall into line behind him, not realizing that my parking brake is still on. My car now smells like burnt rubber. I look in the rearview mirror to see a behemoth of a vehicle, a pickup truck/dump truck/semi-cab with a Superman logo on the front license plate. The rolling five-ton mastodon looks like something out of *Thunderdome*. Shaquille O'Neal is behind the wheel, bobbing his head up and down. The bass coming from his speakers rattles my rearview mirrors. Now *that's* gangsta.

We pull onto the causeway to South Beach. D.J. in front. Shaq on my bumper. After a few miles, I realize my blinker has been on since we made the right off Biscayne Boulevard. Shaq must think I'm a complete tool.

On Collins, next door to Opium Garden, where *The Magazine* hosted a Shaq party three months ago, is a restaurant called La Factoria. Jones glides into a parking space right in front. He gets out and leaves the windows down. I park a few spots away, behind a Ferrari Spider. The valet guys look like they're about to hurl when my Buick pulls to a stop.

Jones and I grab a table on the sidewalk. The waiter rushes over to serve us. He goes for the chicken parmesan. I choose the turkey club. As soon as the waiter leaves I realize my mistake. I should have picked something easier to chew. Like Jell-o.

Shaq and a few of his boys grab the next table over. Jones is now deep in thought. When he talks about his career, he does so in a low, thoughtful voice as if measuring what he says carefully. I have to lean in close to hear the stories about how much it hurts to be cut ten times in one career. About how frustrating life on the NBA's fringe can be.

"What are you writing, a book?"

My interview comes to a halt. Shaq is taking over.

"Can you autograph me a copy?"

The big fella doesn't want Thoughtful D.J. right now. He wants Sidekick D.J.

Jones can see this and he won't let his boy down. "I've got a new nickname for myself," he boasts. "Six to One. Because that's my assist to turnover ratio."

Shaq cracks up. "Yo, D. Jones, you know that new Phantom comes out in September," he says. "I'm thinking about picking one up. Midnight blue convertible with a European steering wheel. You gonna be on the left side when we roll through. May I please have some Grey Poupon?"

"How much does it cost?" asks Jones.

"About $415,000." Shaq mimes opening a briefcase.

"Damn, that's too rich for me. I'll go half with you."

"No way. I'm buying that thing in cash. I'm just going to show up with a shoebox full of money. You know I keep all my cash at my house. That's the best place because that's the first place the stick-up kids come looking. If somebody rolls up like that, I'll be quick to rat-a-tat a motherfucker with them big things because you know I still keep them heaters."

Jones can only shake his head. A passerby shouts, "Good game yesterday, Shaq!"

Shaq nods but doesn't lose his flow.

"You see that condo over there," he says, pointing to an orange high rise a block or so over. "I was going to buy it. Just to get away, but it was only $4 million. I might get it, though. I'm going to

Frank Sinatra that bitch out. Really hook it up. I'd put a door man at every room."

A deeply tanned blonde dressed in aerobic wear and designer sunglasses sidles up to Shaq's table, trying to recruit him for a yoga workout. This gives Jones a window of opportunity to tell me the story about how the Rockets practiced at his high school during his senior year, how he rebounded for Sam Cassell, who took a liking to him. That's why he wears number 19.

"Hey, D. Jones," Shaq says, breaking Jones' train of thought. "How much you want to bet me on the Super Bowl, $50,000?" Kickoff is only a few hours off for the Patriots and the Eagles.

"Slow down," Jones replies. "That's a little out of my league."

"I tell you what, my $10,000 to your $5,000."

"That's a bet. I got Philly. Gotta go with my boy T.O."

"No problem. I got the dynasty. Tom Brady hasn't let me down yet."

"Wait and see. Never sleep on T.O."

"Just make sure you pay up, in cash. Don't forget I know where you live."

"I know where you live, too."

"But I got Rottweilers."

Shaq gets up, thanks the waiter, and leaves with his boys. They don't pay for a thing. Moments later, the monster truck appears. "Six o'clock be at my house," says Shaq. He cranks up the music and does his Merton Hanks imitation behind the wheel. His giant body flails as he laughs, pulling away from the restaurant. His license plate reads BIG BEEZ.

Jones shakes his head and stares at his half-eaten food. He's thinking about the Super Bowl. "You know what's funny?" he asks. "Right this second, as we sit here, the guys are in the locker room getting dressed. Some of them are probably already on the field stretching or running routes. Right now. I mean we're sitting here at this restaurant and they're getting ready to play in the biggest game of their lives."

He's in his own world now. I'll bet he's picturing himself in the locker room getting ready for Game One of the NBA Finals. It's so close, he can taste it. He pulls a crisp $50 bill out of his wallet and weights it down on the table beneath the knife he never used.

HOUSTON, FEBRUARY 9

I'VE NOW FIGURED OUT that the pain in my tooth is linked to my blood pressure. The moment it rises, the agony intensifies. And so I have resorted to taking long deep breaths.

When I got off the plane in Houston, it's a test of will—to reach the baggage claim. George Bush Intercontinental Airport is a gigantic maze. You need to travel by tram, but I can't find one. And thanks to construction, the route to my luggage seems like a quarter mile. I know, a few pages ago I was bragging about how much I love to walk, but this is more than I bargained for. The two laptops in my backpack bow my spinal cord like cinderblocks. *Only seven pounds, my ass.* I have a second bag with a strap flung over my shoulder. All this weight is causing me to labor. My blood pressure is soaring. Why haven't they invented Anbesol-flavored chewing gum?

Breathing long and slow, I have to stop every hundred feet. When I finally arrive at the baggage claim, my bag is going around the carousel all by itself, like a kid whose parents forgot to pick him up after school.

Enough is enough. I decide to cancel the last ten days of my trip and return to New York for surgery. *Damn threshold. Why am I acting so tough? Why am I so lazy even in the face of cataclysmic pain?* I feel a sense of duty. That's it. *Yeah, this book's important.* I need to be out here on the road come what may. And so I'm going to the Rockets-Bulls game tonight. Maybe just a quarter or two. Let's see how I feel at halftime.

Bad move.

Every time the crowd screams, the sound waves go straight into my tooth. I'm praying for the Bulls to catch on fire and quiet this place, but they're getting run out of the gym. Both coaches empty their benches. The crowd cheers even louder for the scrubs.

By game's end, I'm biting my tongue to distract myself, sort of a crude acupuncture kind of thing. Just before the final buzzer, I stumble to the bathroom to spit out a mouthful of blood. I'm in too much pain to move. When I get back to the hotel, I get on the Internet and begin to search for a Houston dentist who subscribes to the company insurance plan. And then I remember the password thing. Isn't there supposed to be something to click on if you forget your password?

I give up.

By the next morning, the pain has eased. Detroit here I come.

DETROIT, FEBRUARY 10

COATESVILLE, PENNSYLVANIA, IS TWENTY-EIGHT miles and a world away from the immaculate yards that lie like giant green floor mats beside the upscale homes of Philadelphia's Main Line, the tree-lined streets where Kobe Bryant lived during his high school days with his mother, father, and two sisters. Up and down the Main Line, daddy's little girls steer their BMW 325s with the kind of entitlement that doesn't require them to use turn signals or throw you a "sorry" wave after they cut you off. But basketball is the great equalizer across the state of Pennsylvania. You can't shut off the baseline with your zip code. You can't raise your field goal percentage by changing the address on your birth certificate.

Kids from Coatesville work hard. They know the value of an honest day's pay. They learn it by watching their parents shuttle back and forth with their lunch buckets from the local steel mills. Not far from the middle class development of Brandywine Homes, where Rip Hamilton was raised by his parents, Richard Sr. and Pamela Long, there are two slabs of asphalt and, rising out of the ground, steel poles with chain link nets on rusty old hoops that always present a hazard to fastbreakers. Here in Ash Park, reps are made and destroyed, depending on whether or not you brought your A-game. The well-worn courts sit in a small valley surrounded by steep grassy hills like a workaday Coliseum. The fact that Rip and his boys had to pass the Oak Street projects to get to the park was just extra incentive to bring it.

Hamilton earned respect from the project ballers by wearing them out. Because you can't beat what you can't catch, he never stopped moving. "He's always been that way," says cousin and one-time teammate Jontue Long. "The way his heart, lungs, and breathing work, it's a gift."

One of the first people to discover that gift was Kobe Bryant, who played with Hamilton on a Philadelphia-area AAU team in the summer of 1995. Tonight at The Palace of Auburn Hills, Kobe's Lakers will square off with Rip's Pistons in a rematch of the 2004 NBA Finals, which the Pistons won in five games to claim Detroit's first title in fourteen years. Only this time, there will be no Shaq. No Phil Jackson. And no Kobe. As the Pistons race out to a 23–4 lead, Kobe watches the slaughter unfold from his seat behind the bench. Wearing a brown corduroy blazer and a pink dress shirt, he tugs nervously at the knees of his pricey pre-faded designer jeans as Rasheed Wallace forces Lamar Odom into a turnover resulting in a Hamilton dunk.

Of the twelve men on the Lakers' active roster, only Luke Walton, Brian Cook, and Slava Medvedenko played on last year's Western Conference Championship team. The Pistons are the sole marquee attraction on this night, leading from tip to buzzer in a 103–81 romp. Four starters score in double figures, with Tayshaun Prince leading the way with 25 points. As the Pistons run away with the game, Kobe stares at the ground. His image is broadcast on the Jumbotron and the crowd begins to boo. He doesn't bother to look up. He's the most hated man in the NBA right now. Not in a love-to-hate kind of way. More like a despised kind of way. Like you-thought-you-were-the-shit-the-way-you-looked-down-at-us-with-your-straight-from-high school-Main-Line-nose-in-the-air-for-so-many-years-but-look-at-you-now sort of thing.

People love to pile on Kobe Bryant. Probably because it once seemed like Kobe had everything. Looks. Money. Game. Raging sense of entitlement. And he knew it. Never really rubbed it in your face, but you could see it in his eyes and hear it in his voice. He knew it. Knew you knew it. And that was a little infuriating for most people. Reporters and players and league officials and shoe reps from Adidas regularly talked behind his back. They shut up when he walked by. No one wanted to get on his bad side.

Shaq—the world's greatest living center—refused to tiptoe around Kobe and he got shipped off to Miami. So how could Kobe's current teammates front like they had no worries? "Some people just stayed out of his way," a former Laker told me. "It was easier. Most of the time he kept to himself, but he was watching you. Watching the way you practiced like he was Jordan or some shit. You couldn't argue with it because you weren't going to win that argument. Everybody upstairs loved Kobe. Even the ones that didn't acted like they did."

These days, Kobe's bad side is not so treacherous. Although the Colorado thing is behind him, he can't flex his muscle like he once did. He's human now and everyone knows it. The only way he's getting back on top is to win people over. That's what any smart person in Kobe's position would be thinking and Kobe Bryant is a smart person. He needs friends in a way he never has before. He has at least one.

The final buzzer sounds and Kobe wades through the flood of players, coaches, ballboys, and security personnel to find Rip Hamilton, coming toward him, unhitching the Velcro straps on his protective facemask. The two embrace for a long time, patting each other on the back, whispering congratulations and what's ups. They step back, exchanging toothy grins, Hamilton's left hand on Kobe's shoulder, Kobe's on the back of Hamilton's head. Never have I seen Kobe so at ease, so openly friendly with an opponent. More shocking still is to see someone else so relaxed around him. Players from other teams are reluctant to fraternize with Kobe, largely because they assume he has no interest in friends. But Kobe wants to shed the loner tag, to be one of the guys. He wants to laugh and joke with his colleagues around the league. For him, though, it's not that simple. Except with Hamilton. With Hamilton, it's easy.

Beatwriters who follow Kobe struggle to name players he counts as friends. They recall attempts to socialize with his teammates outside the walls of the Staples Center or the Lakers practice facility, but scarcely know of anyone who's been to his home. He simply lives too far away.

Hamilton is the right fit for Kobe. His sunny disposition makes it easy for Kobe to be himself, even if he doesn't yet know who that is. Kobe trusts him, refuses to judge him. They have a history.

DETROIT, FEBRUARY 12

I'M DRIVING UP I-75 towards Auburn Hills when I spot the sign for Adams Road. I pull off the exit and loop around to an intersection that gives me the option of going right or left. "Take Adams north until you run into South Boulevard," Josh Nochimson had told me a half hour earlier. Of course, Adams appears to run east to west. The Pistons tip off in thirty-five minutes and I'm running late, but I refuse to let The Confusion Factor rear its ugly head, so I make a left and hope for the best. Five minutes later, I arrive at the two-story townhouse where Nochimson sleeps when he's not running Hamilton's life.

Upstairs in the living room, boxes are everywhere, reminders of the move Nochimson made three months ago. On a small table sits a three-inch stack of unopened mail—tax papers, account statements, official looking stuff—addressed to Richard C. Hamilton. Nochimson's name is engraved on a nearby glass trophy commemorating the 1999 NCAA Basketball Championship won by the University of Connecticut. Hamilton was the star swingman. Nochimson was a team manager.

Nochimson checks a few college box scores on ESPN.com and we jump into a leased silver Audi A6 once owned by Sergie Federov of the NHL. Nochimson promptly plugs his phone into the cigarette lighter, slips on the earpiece with wraparound microphone, and begins sorting out who gets what tickets. His commands are quick and to the point without betraying his endearing nonchalance. "Where are those seats? 103? Listen, get him on the phone. No. Is she coming tonight? Rip's parents are behind the basket. Come on, just do it. Can you believe this?"

He fingers the volume on the stereo, nearly muting *Bruce Springsteen—Greatest Hits*, and gets down to business. His rapid-fire speech is a bit more irritated. Too many tickets, envelopes, seats, sections, requests. Ten minutes later, we pull up to the Palace and Nochimson flashes a laminated card with the words GUEST OF RICHARD HAMILTON at the parking attendant. He waves us into the lot next to the section reserved for players. We walk the twenty yards to the entrance for friends and family. Nochimson slips off the earpiece, if only for a moment, and lets out a sigh. "This is a big game tonight," he says. "Who are we playing?"

These are good times in Motown. The Pistons are making the extra pass. Rasheed Wallace is asserting himself. Antonio McDyess looks three years younger on his feet. Chauncey Billups has harnessed the backspin on his jumpshot. Coach Brown is smiling. With each new day, anticipation builds, bringing the Pistons one step closer to duplicating the feat that shocked the basketball world.

The Wizards are no match, quickly succumbing in a 107–86 rout. "We were really great tonight," Brown says, perusing a dog-eared final box score at his postgame press conference. "Look at that, 33 assists on 43 baskets. Man, we were just great tonight. This is about as good as it gets."

Just after midnight, Hamilton settles into the barber's chair in front of the mirrored wall in the full-service barbershop situated on the second floor of his million-dollar home. His personal barber, James Wilson, trims the scraggly baby hair on his forehead and temples. In walks Hamilton's cousin, Jontue Long, wearing a size fifty-two jersey with the words RIP CITY on the front and COATESVILLE on the back. Rip's assistant, Henry Cooper, who lives in the basement, arrives next, wearing the same jersey, different colors. Before long, nearly a dozen friends from Hamilton's beloved hometown have turned the room into a thirty-by-twenty-eight-foot laugh riot. They tease each other just as they did in Ron's

Barbershop back home, especially Cooper, who once drove a moped through Ron's front window.

"You know A.I. got 60 tonight," someone says to a chorus of disbelief. Hamilton spots Long's jersey. That's Long's version of a tux, he says. Long doesn't disagree. Soon the gang is caught up in a heated debate on the time-honored topic: Tupac vs. Biggie. Hamilton turns 27 tomorrow. The party's tonight and everyone's in town. Then again, when Hamilton's around, they're always close at hand. Thirty minutes later, it seems half of Coatesville is standing on the white marble floor of his two-story foyer. Hamilton towers over everyone, adjusting his ever-present do-rag. "How many people we got?" he asks, trying to count heads. "Fifteen? Sixteen? Seventeen? Who are the designated drivers? How many cars do we need?"

Someone asks if tonight will be fun. "Yes siiiiir," shouts Hamilton, using his personal catchphrase. His pals call it a Coatesville thing. When you hear it, things are going well in the House of Rip. Tonight is a Yes Sir kind of night.

Because the crew is so deep, we have to commandeer Hamilton's entire fleet. The birthday boy throws on his fox fur—complete with real fox heads on the elbows—and jumps in the Maybach he bought last year with the money he got for winning the championship. The license plate reads 04 BONUS.

Long gets behind the wheel of the Bentley coupe. A third driver takes command of the Range Rover. Hamilton lets his sister and her friends drive the Jag. He's owned that car for awhile so he won't be too upset if the bumper comes back dented. I ride with Nochimson in his Audi. As we roll down Woodward Avenue through Birmingham, a leafy suburb not unlike Philadelphia's exclusive Lower Merion, Antonio McDyess pulls his car out of a bank parking lot and cabooses our caravan.

This is how you're supposed to roll.

The street leading to the club that will host Hamilton's party is routinely closed to traffic, barricaded by police officers with orange cones. Hamilton inches the Maybach toward the cones and rolls down the window. A police officer scurries off to move the cones aside and we proceed half a block to the club's entrance. The line to get in winds around the block. Hoochie mamas stand three and four across next to girls who have to get up at seven in the morning and go to work at banks or doctor's offices.

"Are they shooting a rap video or something?" I ask.

"I don't think so," Nochimson replies.

"They need to be."

We quintuple park right in front of the club, which used to be a strip joint, and open our doors in unison. It'd look really cool in slow motion. When the onlookers see Hamilton, they let out a gasp.

"Look at his coat," says one admirer.

Two 300-plus-pound bodyguards emerge from the club's door to escort us inside. We line up single file, one bouncer in front, the other in the rear, and snake our way to the third floor. Scarcely an inch of unoccupied dance floor remains. The club's new owners left the stripper poles up and they're getting plenty of use by young women. I'm sandwiched between Hamilton and McDyess. People reach out to touch them as we walk by.

The bouncers lead us to a VIP area on the top floor. We take cover in a small room way in the back. I'm pretty sure it was once the champagne room. Behind the bar, a mother and daughter team are serving thirsty patrons. I spend most of the night just inside the roped-off VIP area chatting up the Coatesville crew and watching the women vying to crash the party. One in her mid-twenties, dressed in fishnet stockings and a tight black skirt, manages to convince a bouncer that she's a guest. She gets all the way to the tight hallway outside the former champagne room. She can see Hamilton's white do-rag bobbing in the crowd. She whispers something to the bouncer guarding the entrance. He isn't buying it. She'll have to wait for Hamilton to come to her.

She stands for nearly twenty-five minutes with her neck craned skyward, staring intently in Hamilton's direction, willing him to make eye contact with her.

"Do you know Rip?" I ask her.

"Yeah, I met him twice. Once at a mall," she says with confidence. "He definitely remembers me. I'm just waiting for him to come out. We're really good friends."

"If you're such good friends, how come you're standing here?"

She shoots me a frown.

"The bouncer doesn't recognize me. They usually have a different bouncer here."

When the house lights come up, it takes the club's staff nearly half an hour to clear the way for Hamilton's crew. The girls in fishnet's gang are reluctant to leave without any face time. Two bouncers drag one away by the arms. She curses them, telling them that her brother will be back to shoot up the place. Outside in the street, the cars are waiting right where we left them. The police clear a path so we can make a quick getaway up I-75.

Nochimson whips out his phone, going over the last-minute details for tomorrow morning's trip. Hamilton has chartered a jet to fly a dozen of his boys to Connecticut for a 1 o'clock game against North Carolina. They have to wake up in four hours.

"The jet is going to cost us a fortune for one day's use," says Nochimson, taking off his earpiece one last time. "But it truly is the only way to fly."

NEW YORK, FEBRUARY 15

I DROP MY BAGS and I head straight for the dentist. In two days, I'll be in Denver for the All-Star Game and I don't want a nagging ache to spoil the fun. My tooth is beyond repair, the dentist says. The filling has come out, exposing the nerve. The pain has faded because the nerve is dead. My molar is a casualty of war.

Good night, sweet tooth. I have damned you with neglect. May you know no more pain.

DENVER, FEBRUARY 17

AFTER CHECKING INTO THE hotel late on Thursday afternoon, I grab lunch with *Slam* editor-in-chief Ryan Jones. It's sort of a tradition for the *Slam* boys and me to get together at the All-Star Game. In San Francisco back in 2000, a handful of hoop fanatics thrown into the fire, we were an instant hit with the players, who gave us more access after a year on the beat than guys who had been covering the league for half their lives. Some colleagues thought we were the coolest, freshest thing to hit sports journalism. The rest resented us because we could pull off the Spud Webb throwback with the matching Air Force Ones. Back then we were all in our retro jersey phase. More than a few paychecks had been burned at Mitchell & Ness in Philadelphia.

The New Yorker once published a Talk of the Town piece on *Slam's* hip-hop guerilla journalism and someone asked me why I wasn't featured in it.

"Because I don't work for *Slam*," I kindly explained.

I guess we stood out because we were so psyched to be living the NBA life. We knew everything about the league but almost nothing about covering the game. All-Star weekend was an on-the-job vacation.

On our first day in San Fran, we walked out of the hotel and saw then-Spurs forward Mario Elie walking down the street by himself. "Yo, Mario, where's the party at?" I shouted. Elie looked at the wannabee journos almost half his age and a huge smile crossed his face.

In the bar off the player's hotel, I grabbed a seat next to Allen Iverson, who was clutching a bottle of Jack and buying a round of shots for everyone. That's where I pounded my first Jack and Coke. I idolized Iverson, but I wasn't fucking telling him that. The next night, at a party hosted by the NBA Players Association, the weekend's gala event, I found myself standing outside without an invite. As a rookie, I hadn't yet learned how to finagle a highly coveted pass to the ultimate insider affair. I was just about to take an L when Jermaine O'Neal rolled up with his crew. My ticket to ride. With J.O. at my side and the door wide open, I spotted a beautiful young black girl with a blonde wig and a short sequin skirt. Her skin was flawless. She had been eyeing me while I was pressing my face up against the glass. She gave me the "come here" gesture with her seductive index finger. Not two feet from the party, I said, "Later fellas."

She and I were soon in a cab headed down the street to who-knows-where. I didn't care. Up close, she was the Girl Next Door meets Lil' Kim. My mind was racing. Her eyes were hazel. She batted eyelashes longer than Tayshaun Prince. She crossed her legs in the backseat. Her skirt hiked up. I was distracted by her cleavage. She told me her name. I forgot it in thirty seconds.

The conversation was natural. Her breasts were, too. I was cool. I'm not usually cool.

"Where do you want to go?" I asked.

"Anywhere," she said.

Damn, things just got a whole lot better.

"Well." I said, mindlessly spouting off parties I knew about. She interrupted me.

"I'm a girl," she said.

"Don't I know it."

"No, I'm a girl."

Now I was confused.

"What do you mean?"

"I'm a working girl."

My blood froze.

"What's wrong? You don't look happy."

I told the cab driver to bust a U and take me to the player's hotel. He pulled up to the valet zone and I rifled through some crumpled bills, handing him a ten, which barely covered our fifteen-minute fare. I told her that our night was over. She looked disappointed.

"Don't you have anything for me?" she asked.

I gave her my last four dollars.

"Four dollars?" she said, stuffing the bills into a tiny purse that matched her skirt.

She kissed me on the cheek and glanced at the hotel looking for a bigger score. Lamar Odom happened to be walking by. She stopped in mid-sentence, wrapped her arm around his, and whispered in his ear. She was talking fast, trying to close the deal. Odom looked at me like he'd just stolen my girl. He too was struck by her beauty.

He chuckled, never breaking stride, and brushed her off before getting into a car with his buddies. She turned her attention to Gary Payton, coming our way just out of the lobby. I saw the wife of the late Bobby Phills talking to Ray Allen. It was two in the morning. I turned and started toward my hotel.

Oh, to be a rookie again. But then again, not really. In this, my sixth All-Star weekend, I'm glad to be a veteran. I know what I'm doing. I have an invite-plus-three to the Players Association party and I'm on the list for five other parties. I can smell the "girls" a mile away.

At 7:30, I meet up with my good friend Mandy Murphy, the public relations manager for AND1, and head to a billiards tournament hosted by Alonzo Mourning of the Heat and Carmelo Anthony of the Nuggets. The toast of Denver, Melo is presiding over a different party every night this week, from the makeshift pool hall to The Paladium to a strip club called the Oasis Cabaret, which will project his image hour upon hour onto a 6,000-square-foot tent outside the door. For $850, partygoers can secure a four-day pass to Club Melo and walk the red carpet mingling with the likes of A.I., Nelly, and Ludacris.

The red carpet is in full swing when we arrive. We step past the camera crews and hustle inside to find twenty pool tables and a half-dozen bars. Waitresses dressed in skimpy blue outfits peddle shots of a blue liquid called Hpnotiq. Rappers have been mixing it with cranberry juice for about a year now.

I'm still trying to get the lay of the land when a buxom Brazilian girl with an impossibly small waist offers me one.

"Might as well," I say, taking a glass off her tray. I pound it. For courage.

"I like your outfit," I say.

She smiles.

"They told us the material is the equivalent of six feet of toilet paper," she says gleefully. "I could have gone with four."

"I wish you had." *Damn, that was a smooth comeback. The kind of line I usually think of after I have returned to the hotel.*

"You're bad," she says before winking and pushing Hpnotiq on other partygoers.

I'd planned to watch Damon Jones and Udonis Haslem shoot pool against Denver Broncos cornerback Champ Bailey and my *ESPN The Magazine* colleague Carmen Renee Thompson. But the first-round showdown is scheduled to begin in five minutes and Jones is nowhere to be found. I call his cell. Haslem does, too. No answer.

I find myself filling in for D.J. until a suitable replacement can be found.

Bailey breaks and drops a solid ball into a side pocket. He's got his own pool table, which means he knows what he's doing. So does Haslem. And Thompson clearly suckered us into thinking she lacks game. She isn't the Black Widow, but she's Bailey's equal. I suck. Horribly. It's as if I've never played before.

"I don't know what happened. I used to be good," I say. No one buys it. Haslem is starting to smolder. We're getting killed. It doesn't help that the place is jam packed. Our table is right by a major artery to the bathroom.

I chalk up and steady my stick. Gotta show these people something. I...pull...the...cue...back...and drill the rapper Fabolous in the hip.

"My bad, bro."

Fab nods and keeps on moving. To my good fortune, his bodyguard missed the whole thing.

Cedric the Entertainer, who is MCing the party, walks by mic in hand.

"Yo, Ced, give some love to *ESPN The Magazine*," I shout.

"Much props to *ESPN The Magazine*," he says into the microphone.

"Check out the NBA issue with your boy on the cover."

Someone taps my shoulder. I turn around. It's Damon Jones.

"That's it for you. Y'all gettin' killed," he says. "Damn, I got my work cut out for me now. U, why you let this happen? You supposed to represent and you and the writer getting whooped."

Haslem shakes his head. I'm toast. I hand the stick to Jones and head to the bench.

Jones misses his first shot and Bailey proceeds to clear the table. He and Thompson will make it all the way to the final four.

I post up at the bar, pretending to be cool, while nursing my Jack and Coke. Leaning on the rail with my back to the bartender and my elbow propped on the countertop, I spy Vivica A. Fox in a simple pair of jeans and a white blouse. I swear I see a breeze blow her hair back. She's just stunning. Does more with a pair of blue jeans than a Hpnotiq girl half her age does with six feet of toilet paper. She looks directly at me and mouths the word, "Hi."

I freeze. Say hi back. At least, I hope I did. It's loud and I'm sure she can't hear me. When I come to my senses, she's gone. I have to talk to her. What can it hurt? I search the club without success. Order another Jack and Coke. Think about what might have been.

Just after 3 a.m., the house lights come on. The universal signal to scramble like mad to get a phone number. By this point, most guys are willing to lower their standards because they've got a few drinks in them. I'm not feeling that pressure because I'm all about the big picture. All-Star weekend has just begun. I've got two more days to catch up with Vivica A. Fox, so I ride it out with the fellas.

I drop in on a handful of players gathered around a pool table talking junk. Jones and Paul Pierce are squaring off. Their chatter is starting to escalate, the volume going up and up. People stop to look. Pierce is on one side of the table, D. Jones on the other. Dwyane Wade, Wade's best friend Marcus Andrews, Udonis Haslem,

Terrell Owens, Jermaine Dupri, LeBron's boy Richard Paul, and I sit and watch as the smack flies.

"I'm on the best team in the East, what else is there to say?" Jones shouts at his former Celtics teammate as he throws his hands in the air.

"I'm the reason why you in the league," Pierce shouts back. "I told management that I needed a fuckin' entourage."

The table erupts in laughter. Jones frowns. "Whatever, that's some bullshit," he counters rather weakly.

"Look at my résumé," Pierce says, without giving him time to regroup. "It speaks for itself. All-Star four times, 25 a game every damn year. I don't give a fuck about championships as long as I'm getting mine and bustin' yo ass."

"Any nigga can get 25 and 10 on a losing team. So what?"

"Only reason you getting shit is because of the Big Fella. If Shaq wasn't there, you wouldn't be getting half those looks."

"He may open it up, but he don't put the ball in the hole for me, now does he?"

Now Pierce is mad.

"Whatever. I made you. I got triple-teamed every night and you lived off me, too. Fuck you. Fuck you. I've been holding it down for-ever. That's why they call me The Truth."

"I knew you since before you were the fucking Truth. Big deal."

"Your motherfucking teammate gave me that name when I torched him."

"Forty and 14, that's all I got to say. No. 1 in the East, mother-fucker!"

The table erupts in laughter once again. Pierce and Jones pace, stew, brush off the cackling, and then, finally, hug over the table. Just a little good-natured ribbing among friends, but there's a kernel of truth in all smack talk. Everyone knows that.

The two players remain tight. They'll hang out together in a few days, but each was singed by the other's remarks. And yet, as the sparks flew, one of the biggest trash talkers in sports history sat humbly on the corner pocket silent as a church mouse. Terrell Owens looked strangely out of his element, almost like the kid at the lunch table who desperately wants to fit in but refuses to laugh too loud for fear that the taunts will be directed at him. *Well, what are you laughing at?* That's how it usually starts.

DENVER, FEBRUARY 18

OUT PARTY-HOPPING WITH Mandy Murphy, I snag a cab to the Reebok lounge only to find that things are winding down. As we exit, I'm carrying an open can of Red Bull. Without warning, a police officer seizes my arm, trying to wrestle the beverage from me. I jerk it away from her. A much bigger officer rushes to her assistance.

"Sir, please relinquish the beverage container!"

"Fuck you guys!" I shout, quickly calculating the odds that they'll want to arrest me before going home at 3 o'clock in the morning.

"Sir, the can."

I briefly consider pouring it on their shoes. But then I'd have to waste my one phone call explaining the whole ordeal to my editor.

"You owe me $2," I say, surrendering the can. I feel like an outlaw. I'm not. I'm a dork. What the hell was in that Red Bull?

DENVER, FEBRUARY 19

WHEN SNOOP DOGG TOOK the stage at last year's Players Association party in Los Angeles, David Stern and Billy Hunter stood in the wings admiring the show as a heavy cloud of marijuana smoke floated in the air above their heads. This year, the party's planners are hoping for a classier affair. Thousands of dressed-to-impress invitees pass through the convention center's doors to find tables draped in black velvet and elaborate ice sculptures beside each of the dozen bars. Murphy, Elena Bergeron—*The Magazine's* rookie NBA reporter—and I are snacking on finger foods when every head in the place turns.

LeBron James has made his entrance, dressed in jeans and Timberland boots. At his side are his three best friends from Akron, Ohio—Randy, Maverick, and Shorty. They roll everywhere together, calling themselves the Four Horsemen. Each owns a pair of Air Force Ones with little Four Horsemen logos on the heels, compliments of Nike. *Talk about limited edition.* Tonight the foursome dons Four Horsemen letterman jackets with their names embroidered on the front. They also have a fifth wheel: New Orleans Hornets rookie J.R. Smith. Every now and again, LeBron taps him on the shoulder to point something out. J.R. smiles and nods. The rest of the time he stands there with his hands in his pockets.

As far as I know, Smith has no connection to LeBron. They did not go to camp together in high school or play in the same prep all-star game. One wears Nike. The other Adidas. But a few months back, I noticed that LeBron often raises his hands above his head after a big play, palms outward, index fingers and thumbs touching to create a spade. Jay-Z uses this gesture to promote his Roc-A-Fella Records empire. LeBron and Jay are friends. The rapper often calls the player's Horsemen buddies to check up on them. And then, one night on *SportsCenter*, I saw Smith flash the Roc sign, too.

For young players like Smith, being linked to LeBron is the height of cool. Sebastian Telfair showed me LeBron's number in his cell phone when he was a senior in high school. But older guys like to be associated with him, too. When the Four Horsemen left their court-side seats during a playoff game last year, in a move that smelled of desperation, Robert "Tractor" Traylor stepped in LeBron's path to make sure he got a pound. Before boarding a team bus at the Finals, Kobe talked with LeBron for a good two minutes, which is longer than I've seen him talk with almost anyone. "Keep it up," he said, before sending LeBron off with a satisfied smile on his face.

Now there are so many well-wishers crowding LeBron, I find myself craving space. I make my way to the front of the room just as Nelly and the St. Lunatics are claiming the stage. In the player VIP section, Allen Iverson two-steps up a storm to "Hot in Herre." Marcus Camby chats with a league official nearby. Quentin Richardson is whispering in the ear of his fiancée, the recording star Brandy. Behind me, Gilbert Arenas of the Wizards is sporting a small fur. "He looks like he borrowed that coat from his grandmother," quips Bergeron.

I head to a bar for a drink. When I return, I can't find Bergeron. At 5-foot-even, she's easy to lose at NBA parties. I have no trouble, however, spotting my friend Jack Stevens, who handles security for the Wizards. When Tim Thomas played in Milwaukee, Stevens was his personal bodyguard. His duties included living in Thomas' house and driving Thomas' silver Bentley. The two had a falling out when Thomas was traded to the Knicks. So Stevens now lives with the Wizards' Peter Ramos. The 7-foot-3 project from Puerto Rico certainly doesn't own a Bentley.

Stevens stands as stiffly as ever, feet shoulder-width apart, arms folded, eyes darting side to side. If there's a Wizard in the room, he's on call.

"There's Gilbert right over there," I tell him.

"Where?"

I point to the grandmother coat and Stevens takes off in that direction, resuming his stance a few feet away from the guard. Damon Jones is the guard who can really use some help, though. He nearly gets crushed when Shaq's extra-large posse brushes up against the crowd of LeBron worshippers. I believe something similar happened to Donkey in *Shrek 2*.

As soon as the house lights come up, LeBron and his boys make a quick exit, finding a safe perch near the top of the stairs in the lobby where they can watch the revelers spill into the night. LeBron looks like a king on his throne sitting up there, surrounded by his court. But poor J.R. Smith is lost in the fray below.

"What's up, J.R.? Chris Palmer, *ESPN The Magazine*."

"Oh, yeah, I remember you," he says.

We'd met at a few high school all-star games.

"You rolling with LeBron now?"

"That's my man. He said he was down to roll tonight so I wanted to come with him. We're cool. We've been boys for awhile."

Even at 6-foot-6, Smith barely merits a second glance from this crowd—not until LeBron descends from on high to reclaim him.

DENVER, FEBRUARY 20

ACCORDING TO THE NBA, the All-Star Game will be broadcast on radio and TV in 214 countries. If I ran onto the court and caused some sort of disturbance, half the planet would know about it. Better not, though. I fancy my freedom.

Besides, fame has its drawbacks. *The Denver Post* published a map today revealing the best hotels for celebrity spotting. I don't need it. I stumble across Nelly in the hallway between the locker rooms, pulling out the current issue of *The Magazine,* which features him on the cover with Amare Stoudemire. Nelly looks at it in awe.

"That's what's up," he says. "That's what's up."

"Is this the first time you've seen this issue?" I ask.

"Yeah, this is tight. Can I have it?"

"No, my brother. You've got to get your own."

I've promised it to someone else.

I watch the game from a seat behind one of the baskets, not far from the mini-stage where Kelly Clarkson performs her hit single "Since U Been Gone." The All-Stars emerge to a recording of "Solider" by Destiny's Child. When the announcer introduces LeBron, he pauses to hold up the Roc-A-Fella sign. The crowd boos Kobe. Shaq chooses not to shake his hand.

The game itself is forgettable, except for a handful of dunks, an alley-oop slam by Kobe, a reverse slam by Dwyane Wade, and one slam each by Vince Carter and Tracy McGrady, who set themselves up by tossing the ball off the backboard. Allen Iverson takes MVP honors, leading the East to a 125–115 win with 15 points, nine assists and five steals. The only real surprise is the cell phone hidden *a la* James Bond in Shaq's size twenty-two shoe. "It's big, you can take it anywhere, make people look at you," Shaq boasts in the locker room before the game, pointing out the antenna concealed in the toe. "And it prevents muggers. Kick them right in the ass with the Shaq shoe phone."

PHOENIX, FEBRUARY 22

BACK TO REALITY. WHEN I check into the hotel, I'm struck by this overwhelming sense of isolation. No groupies in the lobby. No radio D.J.s breathlessly hyping the next big party. No James Worthy in the elevator. In a span of twelve hours, I've gone from being one of 370 out-of-town media members to being one of two. The *Los Angeles Times'* Clippers beatwriter is the other. When I step into my room, I throw up the Roc-A-Fella sign.

The Clippers face the red-hot Suns tomorrow evening. Tonight, they're free to do what they please. I call Brand at about 3 p.m. to invite him to dinner and get his voicemail. Surprise! At least it's not full. *Call me back, Jack.* I pull the shades and turn off my cell for a quick nap. Three hours later, I wake wondering why my phone hasn't rung. Guess that's what happens when you turn it off. Shit. I check my messages. Brand hasn't called.

I give him another shout. *Let's go, dude, I'm getting hungry over here.* I sit down to answer a few e-mails. Two hours pass. Still no Brand. I drive to Long John Silver's and order the chicken platter. Now that's living.

PHOENIX, FEBRUARY 23

EITHER THE CLIPPERS ARE slow tonight or Phoenix is damn fast. This is the first time this season I've seen the Suns and their fastbreak is every bit as good as people say. Rebounds, turnovers, baskets, jumpballs—these guys run off everything. The ball barely touches the ground.

Shawn Marion, Joe Johnson, and Quentin Richardson are well-schooled in spreading the floor, forcing the Clippers defenders to cover more ground than they'd like. On one break, Richardson catches a quick pass and swoops in for a one-handed tomahawk, bringing the fans out of their seats. He gives L.A.'s bench a good-natured woof as he runs back up the floor.

After spending four years in a Clippers uniform, Richardson savors his life on the outside. Unlike Keyon Dooling and Darius Miles, though, he doesn't feel the need to take shots at his former employer. He remains close to a handful of his old teammates, including third-year center Chris Wilcox, who visited the house Richardson shares with Brandy the night before for pizza and a round of video games. As a rookie, Wilcox often found himself chained to Mike Dunleavy's doghouse. Richardson has always done what he can to raise the young center's spirits. But two points in four minutes of play can't be cured with pepperoni.

The Clips guards aren't faring much better. On several occasions, Brand has to surrender his position in the paint to chase down their passes. The Phoenix defenders quickly double down on him, forcing him to pass the ball back outside or select a tougher shot.

Nothing irks Dunleavy more than sloppy fundamentals. That's why these Clippers are usually a sound bunch, like Larry Brown's back-to-back playoff teams of the early Nineties. Why fourth-year forward Bobby Simmons—with his steel drivin' body and John Henry work ethic—averages thirty-seven minutes a game. He rarely takes risks—which allows Dunleavy to keep what little hair he has left.

On this night, however, the coach keeps leaping off the bench to drop F-bombs as the Suns sucker the Clippers into running with them. The result is a 118–101 loss—the eighth of the team's dreaded nine-game road trip. With eight weeks to go, the 23–31 Clippers are six and a half games removed from the eighth and final playoff spot.

When the doors to the Suns locker room swing open, I head straight for center Amare Stoudemire, who's enjoying a breakout season on the team with the league's best record. His peers in the NBA have taken to text messaging each other to rave about his Biblical dunks.

"Excuse me, Amare," I say. "Can you tell me what you think about the Clips? Are they starting to turn things around?"

Sitting knee-deep in a tub of ice water, he turns his head ever so slightly and looks at me like I'm crazy. From the locker to his left, Bo Outlaw calls me out. "Young fella, don't talk until he's had a shower," he chides. "You must be new around here."

The Suns chuckle. I feel like a damned rookie.

"No problem," I shoot back. "I just wanted to ask Amare about your triple double."

Walter McCarty is walking toward the showers carrying a bag of toiletries. He laughs out loud.

"Aw, man," he says, shaking his head.

Oops, my bad, Bo. Triple doubles are for real players.

To be fair, though, Outlaw is just looking out for his boy. No harm in that.

Brand is signing autographs for a few young guys in Suns T-shirts when I find him. He's about to board the team bus.

"Yo, C, what up?" he asks.

"Nothing. Did you get my message? I was trying to hit you up for dinner."

"You know what? My cell went dead and I didn't have my charger. My mom couldn't even get in touch with me. My bad."

No way I can get mad at Mr. Dependable, not after he promises to make amends by spending time with me in L.A. So I leave the arena cursing myself instead—for wearing a brand new pair of Air Jordans on a rainy day.

PHOENIX, FEBRUARY 24

I'M NO GOOD AT getting out of bed—except on travel days. When I'm leaving a city, I can spring off the mattress at four in the morning because I know it's a lot easier to deal with a few groggy minutes than a missed flight or rush-hour traffic.

Today, I'll be traveling by car from Phoenix to Los Angeles. No better way to see the country up close. I jump on the I-10 for the straight shot to my hotel in Santa Monica. An hour later, I'm in the middle of the desert with the sun rising up in the rearview mirror. I'm making great time, cruising at 110 miles per hour. Feeling good, too.

When I'm alone in the car like this, I like to think out loud. Kind of sort out the thoughts in the old noggin. After about 200 miles, I'm in a groove, singing out loud to the Wu-Tang Clan. Oh, all right, so it was Kelly Clarkson.

What a great movie moment this would make:

EXT. ARIZONA DESERT—MORNING
A red Nissan Maxima races like a bullet across the landscape. The driver, a ruggedly handsome sportswriter, clutches the steering wheel, his head bobbing from side to side.

SPORTSWRITER (singing off key):
"Since you been gooone! YEAH! I can breathe for the first time!"

Cut and print.

Damn, I should be in pictures.

EASTERN CONFERENCE

ATLANTIC DIVISION

	W	L	PCT	GB	HOME	ROAD	LAST–10	STREAK
Boston	29	28	.509	–	19–9	10–19	6–4	Won 2
Philadelphia	26	29	.473	2	15–11	11–18	5–5	Lost 3
New Jersey	25	32	.439	4	16–12	9–20	5–5	Won 2
Toronto	24	32	.429	4.5	18–11	6–21	5–5	Won 3
New York	24	33	.421	5	17–12	7–21	6–4	Won 3

CENTRAL DIVISION

	W	L	PCT	GB	HOME	ROAD	LAST–10	STREAK
Detroit	35	19	.648	–	20–7	15–12	9–1	Won 7
Cleveland	31	24	.564	4.5	21–6	10–18	5–5	Lost 3
Chicago	29	24	.547	5.5	18–10	11–14	7–3	Won 2
Indiana	28	27	.509	7.5	16–121	2–15	7–3	Lost 1
Milwaukee	23	31	.426	12	16–11	7–20	6–4	Won 1

SOUTHEAST DIVISION

	W	L	PCT	GB	HOME	ROAD	LAST–10	STREAK
Miami	42	16	.724	–	23–5	19–11	8–2	Won 2
Washington	31	24	.564	9.5	21–8	10–16	5–5	Lost 2
Orlando	28	27	.509	12.5	19–8	9–19	3–7	Lost 3
Charlotte	11	42	.208	28.5	9–18	2–24	1–9	Lost 3
Atlanta	10	45	.182	30.5	8–19	2–26	1–9	Lost 8

WESTERN CONFERENCE

SOUTHWEST DIVISION

	W	L	PCT	GB	HOME	ROAD	LAST–10	STREAK
San Antonio	43	13	.768	–	24–2	19–11	7–3	Won 1
Dallas	38	17	.691	4.5	19–10	19–7	8–2	Won 1
Houston	32	24	.571	11	18–12	14–12	7–3	Lost 3
Memphis	31	25	.554	12	18–10	13–15	5–5	Won 1
New Orleans	11	45	.196	32	8–18	3–27	3–7	Lost 4

NORTHWEST DIVISION

	W	L	PCT	GB	HOME	ROAD	LAST–10	STREAK
Seattle	38	16	.704	–	20–8	18–8	7–3	Lost 1
Minnesota	28	29	.491	11.5	16–13	12–16	4–6	Won 1
Denver	27	29	.482	12	16–9	11–20	7–3	Won 3
Portland	22	32	.407	16	14–12	8–20	4–6	Lost 1
Utah	19	37	.339	20	12–16	7–21	4–6	Won 2

PACIFIC DIVISION

	W	L	PCT	GB	HOME	ROAD	LAST–10	STREAK
Phoenix	43	14	.754	–	20–7	23–7	7–3	Lost 1
Sacramento	36	21	.632	7	20–8	16–13	4–6	Won 2
L.A. Lakers	28	27	.509	14	19–11	9–16	4–6	Lost 3
L.A. Clippers	25	32	.439	18	19–10	6–22	2–8	Lost 1
Golden State	16	39	.291	26	11–18	5–21	4–6	Lost 1

MONEY CHANGES EVERYTHING

CHICAGO, MARCH 1

NOT SINCE MICHAEL JORDAN and Scottie Pippen played in Chicago have the Bulls been this close to the playoffs. With seven weeks to go in the season, they exude a steely confidence—even against a star like Tracy McGrady.

Thirty-seven seconds into tonight's game, that all changes. On a drive to the hoop, Luol Deng crashes to the floor in pain. In the second quarter, an intern from the team's public relations department ambles down press row with the following bulletin.

PLAYER: LUOL DENG

INJURY: RIGHT ANKLE SPRAIN

STATUS: WILL NOT RETURN

Out on the court, McGrady backs Kirk Hinrich down for an uncontested hoop. At 6-foot-3, Hinrich has neither Deng's height nor his quickness. McGrady swats him away like an annoying horsefly. He finds Yao Ming in the paint with a no-look pass that rattles the rim. The floodgates are open. The Bulls get swamped, 119–89.

After the game, Deng emerges from the trainer's room on crutches, sheepishly shaking his head. He smiles that toothy grin, clearly embarrassed by the final score. "It feels better already," he says of the ankle. "It really scared me at first because it happened so fast. I wish I could have been out there to help my teammates."

He pauses for a moment, shifting his weight ever so slightly on the crutches.

"That was pretty bad, huh?"

"Yeah, that was bad. That was real thin."

NEW YORK, MARCH 9

OFF ON A FISHING expedition at Madison Square Garden, I engage in a little light conversation with Brendan Haywood and Laron Profit, two of Rip Hamilton's old Washington Wizards teammates. Between stories about Hamilton's myriad talents and the challenge of playing with Jordan, one word keeps popping up.

Window.

Talk to anyone in the NBA long enough and you'll hear about *the window*—the narrow span of time a player has in which to establish himself. Once your window closes, you're out of luck. With exquisite genetics and hard work, you can sometimes keep it open until you turn 30—33 if you're an all-time great. But windows often slam shut at 25. For a 23-year-old starter, that's sobering news. Better make a quick impression, because you never know who the GM is going to draft next summer. In 1995, Penny Hardaway was a first-team, All-NBA point guard, an immensely likeable teammate, one of the original Next Jordans. A year later, Shaq left Orlando for the Lakers and Hardaway tore cartilage in his knee. In a flash, Allen Iverson, Kobe Bryant, and Tim Duncan had blossomed into NBA stars. Then Tracy McGrady, Vince Carter, and Steve Francis. By 2000, Hardaway's knees were so bad that he could barely climb the stairs after practice. Coaches no longer gameplanned for him. He was coming off the bench in Phoenix, notching 12 points a game for a losing team. No one cared.

Injuries hastened Hardaway's fall, but consider this: In 2002, Kobe Bryant was the game's hottest player. He'd won three NBA titles in a row. Then he made that ill-fated trip to Colorado, the Cavaliers drafted LeBron James, and Shaq left Los Angeles for Miami. Just like that, Kobe's reign was over. That's how quickly things change.

I first heard of the window in my days as a cub reporter. As soon as I shut off my tape recorder, players would say, "'Cause you know my window is closing" or "Can't miss your window." This has little to do with feeding one's family, as Latrell Sprewell once foolishly suggested. It's about getting a payday so big you never have to worry about money again.

Players don't like to talk about the window in the press because it makes them sound like baseball's Rickey Henderson, a future Hall of Famer who played a 30th professional season in San Diego with the minor league Surf Dawgs because he couldn't bear to hang up his spikes. That doesn't mean NBA guys aren't concerned about their windows. In fact, they obsess about them.

This is what killed the 2002–2003 Clippers, arguably the most talented team Donald Sterling's franchise has ever assembled. I successfully pitched a cover story on them for *The Magazine's* NBA preview issue. The team imploded one month later. Why? Because four otherwise unselfish guys were playing for maximum contracts. They quickly stopped making the extra pass because the more they had the ball in their hands, the better their odds of scoring security.

Now, coaches hate selfish goals, but they make sense. General managers reward big numbers, right? And so I continued to hear the gripes of guys who were playing for big contracts. They bitched about point guards who wouldn't get them the ball and coaches who sacrificed wins to improve their draft position. A veteran player even confronted one such coach in the parking garage after a game. The coach nearly shit himself. Thereafter he was genuinely afraid of the player and the whole team knew it. The vet got his minutes and a big payday from another team. The coach was fired.

After the Wizards' 93–83 loss to the Knicks, I retire to Jay-Z's 40/40 club in Manhattan for a Captain and Coke with way too much Captain. On the mega screen TV behind the bar, 19-year-old J.R. Smith throws down a spectacular dunk. Across the Hudson River, Charlotte is mounting a furious comeback versus New Jersey. As Smith backpedals downcourt, he throws up the Roc-A-Fella sign.

Man, check out the window on that kid.

MIAMI, MARCH 10

I'M STARTING TO BUY into this Heat championship thing. After making short work of the Minnesota Timberwolves, 107–90, Stan Van Gundy's team looks damn near invincible. Kevin Garnett put up monster numbers—22 points and 19 rebounds—but even Van Gundy defends Miami's defense. "I say this all the time and I mean it, you're not going to stop Kevin Garnett," he says. "But we made him think tonight. We were able to take him out of his rhythm."

MIAMI, MARCH 12

THE HEAT ARE CRUISING along, demolishing one foe after another. The Nets are in a dogfight with Orlando for the eighth and final playoff spot in the East. So let me save you the suspense: When the two teams meet for a Sunday matinee, the Nets fold quickly, 90–65. Not what I'd call an instant classic, but, hey, I'm not complaining. I'm out of the gym by 4 p.m. and Miami sure beats New York in March.

I decide to go for a spin in my Buick LaCrosse. Shit is so gangsta. Creeping along Collins Avenue in the slow, eighteen-block car show that leads to the Marriott, I do a little sightseeing. What's up with the parade of ass—did a Trick Daddy video just let out?

I try sitting a little low and a bit to the left, until I realize how ridiculous I look. I'm not 21 anymore and the dude behind me is driving a yellow Ferrari. When I straighten up, I spy a black Chrysler 300 with matching deep dish 22s coming at me in the opposite lane. I'd know that car anywhere. As it passes, I shout, "Marcus!" The driver, Dwyane Wade's best friend, sitting a little low and a bit to the left, doesn't hear me. Neither does D. Wade, the passenger.

I pick up my cell and dial Marcus' number.

"Yo, I just saw you."

"Where you at?"

"On Collins, a couple blocks in the other direction. What are y'all doing tonight?"

Marcus promises to call me as soon as he knows their plans.

I watch Duke dismantle North Carolina State in the Atlantic Coast Conference Tournament while Miss Nikki—the woman I bumped into at the Staples Center—talks at light speed into my cell phone about what happened at Skybar last night. *That Christian Bale is really something, isn't he?* I tell her I've got to go, time to get ready to hang out with the fellas. I still haven't heard from Marcus so I give him a ring. He picks up right away.

"You guys figure out what you're doing tonight?" I ask.

"We're still at the hotel," he replies.

"OK, I'm just here chillin'. Give me a call when you roll out."

"You bet."

I jump in the shower and check my phone. No message. An hour later still nothing. I get the picture. Here's the problem: You can't just cold call one of your friends at 10:30 on a Saturday night and expect them to have no plans. But there's no way I'm wasting this tropical clime. I call for my Buick. Kill a half hour behind the wheel, then stop to get a bite at this cool Brazilian takeout joint. Get back in the car and steer past Wet Willie's to see which NBA types are hanging out in the sidewalk seating. There are always a few. That's a tip I learned from a Colombian model who's bent on marrying a ballplayer. Doesn't matter which sport.

The hostess with the leopard bikini bottoms is there, but no D. Wade. I'm ready to call it a night. On Collins Avenue, I spot a Rolls-Royce coming toward me. I'd know *that* car anywhere. In the driver's seat, sitting low and a little to the left, a gigantic dude with a black fedora bobs his shaved head.

"Shaq!"

He doesn't hear me.

I don't bother to call.

LOS ANGELES, MARCH 22

REMEMBER MY LIST? THE one with the things I must avoid at all costs. Well, I've permanently surrendered a tooth and I barely staved off arrest in Denver by relinquishing my can of Red Bull. This morning, I am determined to put in a few solid hours of writing before spending the night engaged in the pursuit of some social endeavor. Probably the pursuit of Miss Nikki. I am really cooking on a great entry about T-Mac when nature sends me a text message: Dude, you need to pee. I hit save and set my seventeen-inch PowerBook on one of the pillows on the bed.

When I return to retrieve it, I stop dead in my tracks.

My PowerBook is on its side. On the floor. The screen's blank. The hard drive is making this awful noise. Not the usual smooth whizzing, but a grinding sound. With some clicking, too. And a little bit of scraping.

I'm in trouble. I haven't backed up my work since New Year's Day.

I lift up the computer, press down on the Power On button, and hold it for five long seconds. According to the manual, this is supposed to perform some kind of electronic CPR.

No response.

I'm starting to get nervous.

I put the computer on the desk and begin to pace. Three months' worth of work will be dead and buried if I can't get this thing breathing.

CLEAR!!!

I can hear the voices of the people in my life telling me, "You should back up your work once a week." My editor. My mother. Miss Nikki. Even the valet. Clearly I've been playing chicken with my life. I had planned to back up the manuscript, really I did. Tomorrow?!? As soon as I finished this chapter. When I returned to the office in New York. I always seem to have an excuse.

The room is boiling. I forgot to turn up the A.C. on my way back from the bathroom. Beads of sweat dot my forehead. My hands start to shake. I want to scream, curse somebody, anybody, the man who invented lofty, four-foot-high beds, but I can't. How strange. I'm usually very good at pointing a finger. I must have no one else to blame.

The phone rings.

Who the hell is it?

I look at the caller I.D. Elton Brand.

I storm to the bathroom, sit on the toilet tank, feet on the seat as if I'm holed up on a park bench, take a deep breath, hit TALK.

"E.B., what up?" I say, as calmly as I can. "Where you at?"

"I got a bowling event for the Clippers. I forgot to tell you. I'm driving down to Long Beach right now."

Long Beach? We're supposed to meet today.

"Don't worry about it. I'm here at the hotel working on some stuff. I'll just chill."

"For real?" Brand says. "Why don't you go out and do something?"

"Yeah, yeah, that's what I'll probably do."

"We'll get up tomorrow," he says. "No doubt."

Not if you read about me in the paper first.

After waiting in line at the Apple Store for forty-five minutes, one of the whiz kids at the Genius Bar informs me that my hard drive has to be replaced. I swallow hard.

"How much is that going to cost?"

"About $300."

"How long will it take?"

"If you leave it with us today, we can put it on priority status. Two days tops."

Of course, priority has its price. But I don't care. I'm only in L.A. for three more days.

"I just need my work."

"Uh, we don't specialize in data recovery. If we replace the hard drive, it's like buying a new computer. It won't have any of the software you installed."

That's not good. I can hear my editor's head hitting the floor when I tell him there's no book. Time for a Plan B. The Genius gives me a list of Mac specialists. I race to a data recovery specialist on Pico Boulevard. He looks like a 12 year old hiding behind a devil's beard.

He can recover the lost chapters, he says, slowly stroking the whiskers on his chin, and replace the fried hard drive before I leave town.

The job will cost me $1,000.

My life's in the hands of a geek with an Incredible Hulk T-shirt.

I surrender my laptop and turn to leave. He goes back to his comic book.

LOS ANGELES, MARCH 24

"I DON'T SEE IT," I say, turning left off Sunset Boulevard. "Oh, there it is. I'll be right up."

I'm meeting Brand in the West Hollywood offices of his new company. Like everyone else in L.A., he's taken a keen interest in entertainment. Unlike most everyone else, though, he's got the money to do something about it. And so, together with Steve Marlton, who owns the hot new nightclub Pearl, he's started Gibraltar Entertainment and Production (as in "Rock of").

As usual, I'm lost. I pull up to what I think is Brand's garage entrance, but the gate doesn't raise. Already late, I'm not the mood for any more aggravation. I'm tempted to floor it. Let security take issue. I can't call Brand back. I don't want to look like an idiot. *Did you hear the one about the reporter who couldn't find the garage door on the side of a building?* I return to Sunset, eke my way through traffic to another entrance. Must be the right place. Elton's Escalade EXT is parked on the rooftop lot.

E.B. meets me at the door with his security card. He gives me a quick tour of the digs, winding up at Marlton's office, which looks out across the street at The Roxy, a legendary rock club. From the looks of things, he just moved in. Against one wall on the floor sits a framed Team USA jersey from Brand's trip to the Goodwill Games.

"Hey, Steve, this is my boy Chris," Brand says. "He's the one who's writing the book."

An enormous man, probably in his late thirties, perhaps an athlete 300 pounds ago, gets up from behind the desk. His navy blue golf shirt is stretched beyond repair at the neck and sleeves. He gives me a hearty welcome, but eyes me suspiciously when he thinks I'm not looking. He's not aware that I've got Magic Johnson's peripheral vision.

Brand and I retreat to an office at the other end of the hallway. He tells me he met Marlton, a huge sports fan, on the club scene and the two became fast friends. Marlton owns a string of nightclubs, which have earned him an entrée into Hollywood. The moment a movie exec sets foot in one of his establishments, he's treated like a king. According to Marlton, a studio head once flew to Montana for Christmas aboard his private jet. "People remember things like that," he says. "So the next time I need a favor, I know I'll be taken care of."

Pearl on North Robertson in West Hollywood is the new talk of the town. Usher christened the place with his 25th birthday party. According to a local nightlife web site, the club features "translucent shadow boxes in which erotic dancers grind to the music," "sexy vaudeville acts," and "'Karaoke from Hell,' which offers patrons a chance to test their pipes by fronting a live band." Thanks to the display screens scattered throughout the club, partygoers can dine on macadamia-crusted mahi-mahi and New Zealand rack of lamb with goat cheese au gratin without fear of missing the action.

Marlton and Brand plan to turn Gibraltar into a mini DreamWorks. I'm always skeptical when players try to make the crossover into business, especially in entertainment. Most athletes have no head for numbers beyond individual stats and inflated bank accounts. Their names give them clout in the boardroom, but their crazy schemes rarely advance past mission statements. Magic Johnson owns a successful chain of movie theaters and Starbucks coffee shops. Latrell Sprewell sells high-performance equipment for luxury cars at 310 Motoring. And Steve Francis has a successful clothing line called We-R-One. But MVP.com, the failed sports merchandise web site owned by Michael Jordan, John Elway and Wayne Gretzky, is the more common scenario.

Gibraltar recently wrapped a comedy called *Bottom's Up*, starring Paris Hilton and Jason Mewes, and will soon set to work on a Vietnam War drama titled *Rescue Dawn*, starring Christian Bale and Steve Zahn. Brand prides himself on the company's versatility, the ability to produce popcorn fare for the mainstream audience and serious stuff for the film crowd.

"Good luck with the book," says Marlton as Brand and I head for the door. I get in my car and follow Brand down Sunset. We're off to the recording studio he owns with Snoop Dog. Fountain Avenue offers the best route, but Brand passes on that plan. "I know it's faster," he says. "But I like Sunset. I like to see what's going on."

He drives quickly but not aggressively. He signals once, maybe twice, for every lane change and doesn't hesitate to let someone out of a driveway with a wave. We stop at a Mobil at La Brea. I run in and buy a soda while Brand pumps his own gas. He goes with the 93 octane at $2.92 a gallon. Ten minutes later, we arrive at a nondescript one-story building in Hollywood. There's a young rapper outside wearing an Astros throwback. His name is Trigger and he just signed with Brand's label. He's got a bottle of Windex in one hand. The other is scrubbing the blacked-out windows to earn studio time. That's the way things work around here. If a young artist isn't behind the mic, he's put to work.

Brand and I snake our way to the control center. A stocky man in his mid-thirties greets us at the door with his baseball cap cocked to one side. L.T. Hutton has worked with Tupac, Bone Thugs-n-Harmony, and Snoop Dogg. We step inside his lair and Brand slouches down on a wall-to-wall-length leather couch. I pull up a chair in front of the soundboard and Hutton gives me a crash course in production, walking me through the dozens of knobs, buttons, and slides stretched out before him. He powers up dual G5 towers and scans through scores of files and tracks on two twenty-three-inch flat-screen monitors. "Now we have all this stuff backed up, of course," he says. "It's actually backed up four and five times because I don't take chances." He scoots back in his chair and points to a portable auxiliary hard drive under the soundboard.

This is what it's come to—hip-hoppers are teaching me about responsibility.

"You want to hear a couple tracks?"

"You bet."

He opens a series of screens, trying to locate some things he put together for Snoop to approve. I see a folder labeled Kayla Pictures.

"What's that?"

"That's our newest R&B artist," he says. "She's gonna be the next biggest thing to hit the music scene."

He clicks on a few of her pictures. What a seductress.

"We're bringing her along slowly. We don't rush our artists here," Hutton says. "She's still got some work to do. We want her to drop at just the right time."

He plays a couple of tracks for me, raising the volume with a lever on the soundboard. I can feel wind coming from the floor-to-ceiling speakers five feet in front of us. I look over at the couch to find Brand dozing to a beat that's jet-engine loud. The door to the studio swings open and Hutton shuts off the music. Snoop has arrived. Hutton gets up to greet the legendary rapper.

"What was that you had bumpin' up in here?" Snoop asks. "A pimp could work with that." He turns to me and extends his hand. "What up, lil' nephew?"

"I'm Chris from ESPN," I say. "What's goin' on?"

"Just keepin' things crackin'."

Snoop and Brand hug as Snoop's crew files in. Included among them is New England Patriots linebacker Willie McGinest—a fellow Long Beach native. The smell of marijuana is thick in the air. Snoop's hair is twisted as usual into two long braids. He's wearing a gold chain with a pendant that features two canines doing it doggy style. He just left the set of the movie *The Longest Yard*, where he listened to the single Nelly recorded for the soundtrack.

"My nephew Nelly was laying that shit down," he says. "I'm looking for a beat like that. What you got for me L.T.?"

Hutton clicks through his files, searching for something to play for Snoop. Brand taps my shoulder.

"This is Kayla," he says, introducing me to the girl from the photos. She's a stunner in person, too. Perhaps I should interview her for the book. Cover all my bases, ya know?

Brand sees right through me.

"She's 15," he says. "The girl can sing. She's gonna be huge."

Excuse me while I step out into traffic.

Hutton unveils a smooth, jump-in-the-lowrider-and-hit-Crenshaw type of beat for Snoop, who looks like he's been transported to another world. "That's that shizzle," he says, drifting off to a corner, where he puts his head down, slowly moving it from side to side.

We listen to tracks for forty-five minutes. Trigger enters the studio to ask Hutton where he should put an old couch. One of Snoop's boys lights up and offers me a hit. I decline, but ask him about his Nikes. He tells me about a specialty shoe store on Melrose just before La Brea. I look to the couch. Brand is nowhere to be found.

No sweat. Snoop's talking music. Over one bass-heavy track, he and I bob our heads in unison. He reaches out a hand and I clap him five. I try to picture him back in 1996, laying down "2 of Amerikaz Most Wanted" with Tupac. I think I'm getting a contact high.

Brand eventually returns to fetch me, steering me down the hall to a small soundproof room so we can get on with the interview. I open with a few simple questions, hoping to soften him up just enough to find out how he really feels about returning to the Clippers. He's adept at delivering the company line. "We're gonna turn this thing around…" But I know for a fact that you can repeat that phrase like a mantra without believing it. Quentin Richardson didn't buy it. Keyon Dooling didn't either. And Darius Miles sure as hell didn't.

That's perfectly reasonable when you work for Donald Sterling.

Born Donald Tokowitz to Jewish immigrants in Chicago in 1936, Sterling grew up in the Boyle Heights section of East L.A. In the Fifties, while making his way through Southwestern University School of Law, he made ends meet by working as a salesman for Harry Stein's Coliseum Furniture, a short distance from the future home of the L.A. Sports Arena. He changed his name to Sterling because he wanted people to associate him with quality. One day, he walked into the office and simply said, "My name is Donald Sterling." From then on, it was.

He dumped the money he made as a personal injury lawyer in the Sixties and Seventies into cheap Beverly Hills apartment buildings, which he sat on forever. "I always think long term," he told *Los Angeles Magazine* in 1999. "That's why I have never sold anything that I've purchased. And I never purchase anything I don't think I'm going to keep for a lifetime."

In a delicious slice of irony, Sterling bought eleven apartments near the beach in Santa Monica from his pal and fellow sports enthusiast Jerry Buss. With Sterling's money, Buss bought the Los Angeles Lakers in 1979.

In 1981, Sterling followed suit, snapping up the then-San Diego Clippers from Irv Levin for $12.7 million. Three years later, he thumbed his nose at NBA protocol and moved the team onto Buss' turf without permission. It was the first real mess to confront a young NBA commissioner by the name of David Stern. Sterling mopped the floor with him. He won the right to move the Clips into Buss's backyard, housing them in the dank L.A. Sports Arena, which Hollywood's celebrities treated like public access cable. The Forum was network primetime.

To this day, you can find Sterling front row and mid-court at every game. With his tanned, leathery skin and easy smile, his white pants and cashmere sweaters, it's hard to miss him. But the moment play stops, the man disappears like a guy who's allergic to microphones and TV cameras. Members of the Clippers PR staff struggle to recall his last interview.

In the arena of philanthropy, he's always visible, shuttling here and there to collect Man of the Year Awards the way Lance Armstrong racks up Tour de France trophies. Because of his real estate dealings, he's a hard-nosed negotiator. He just can't see the wisdom in forking over top-shelf salaries for talented young players.

In the fall of 2000, Sterling's Clippers had a remarkable roster: Keyon Dooling, Corey Maggette, Darius Miles, Lamar Odom, Michael Olowokandi, Quentin Richardson. Five seasons later, all but Maggette are gone. In the end, stingy Sterling always has an out. He can argue that the team's talent just didn't develop, that the players— not the organization—squandered their potential. Miles was shipped to Cleveland and Olowokandi, Richardson, Odom, and Dooling left via free agency. The stage was set for yet another Clippers revival.

"Yeah the losing gets tiring," says Brand. "It's nothing you can get used to. Always missing the playoffs, being on the outside looking in come March, it's not cool. I don't know how much more I can take. But when I start feeling like that, I just think about what it's going to be like to play with a point guard like Shaun Livingston. He's a one-of-a-kind player and it gives you hope for the future."

The Clippers' new draft pick is well worth raving about. After recovering in mid-season from a dislocated kneecap and torn cartilage in his shoulder, he has exhibited the kind of poise you expect to find in a big-brother-little-brother matchup out on the driveway. But how much can you build on that?

Brand freely admits he has no special insight into the Clippers' front office plans. All summer long, free agents pressed him for info on Sterling's commitment to winning and Brand could only reply, "I see what you see. You have to decide for yourself."

"What about making another run at playing in Miami?" I ask him. "By then, Shaq will have retired and you and Dwyane Wade would make a great one-two punch."

He sinks back into the leather couch, stares straight ahead, and smiles. It's a sweet thought. He rubs his chin with his left hand. The smile fades. No answer.

He's due back at Gibraltar for a 6 o'clock meeting. We emerge from the room and make our rounds, bidding the crew a fond farewell.

"Call me later, C," Brand says. "We'll do something tonight."

"Sure," I reply, heading for the door. On the way out, I peer into a room to find Snoop talking on an out-of-date telephone. You know, the kind with an actual dial. Some ancient rocker probably had it installed.

Drop it like it's 1970.

THE PLAYOFF PICTURE

EASTERN CONFERENCE

	W	L	PCT	HOME	ROAD	LAST—10	STREAK
1. Miami	54	19	.740	32—5	22—14	7—3	Lost 1
2. Detroit	44	27	.620	27—9	17—18	6—4	Won 1
3. Washington	40	30	.571	25—9	15—21	7—3	Won 3
4. Chicago	40	31	.563	23—13	17—18	8—2	Won 8
5. Boston	38	33	.535	25—12	13—21	6—4	Lost 4
6. Cleveland	37	33	.529	26—9	11—24	4—6	Lost 1
7. Indiana	37	34	.521	21—14	16—20	6—4	Won 2
8. Philadelphia	35	36	.493	20—14	15—22	6—4	Lost 2
Orlando	34	37	.479	23—12	11—25	3—7	Won 2
New Jersey	34	38	.472	20—16	14—22	7—3	Won 2
New York	29	41	.414	21—14	8—27	3—7	Lost 4
Toronto	29	42	.408	21—13	8—29	3—7	Lost 2

WESTERN CONFERENCE

	W	L	PCT	HOME	ROAD	LAST—10	STREAK
1. Phoenix	54	17	.761	25—9	29—8	7—3	Won 3
2. San Antonio	53	18	.746	34—3	19—15	6—4	Won 3
3. Seattle	49	22	.690	24—12	25—10	7—3	Lost 1
4. Dallas	48	23	.676	24—12	24—11	8—2	Won 3
5. Houston	44	28	.611	22—13	22—15	7—3	Won 2
6. Sacramento	44	29	.603	27—10	17—19	5—5	Lost 1
T. Denver	39	31	.557	25—10	14—21	8—2	Won 1
T. Memphis	39	31	.557	22—13	17—18	5—5	Lost 3
Minnesota	38	34	.528	21—15	17—19	7—3	Won 5
L.A. Lakers	33	38	.465	22—15	11—23	1—9	Lost 1
L.A. Clippers	32	40	.444	25—13	7—27	5—5	Lost 3

LIMPING DOWN THE STRETCH

MIAMI, APRIL 5

A DATE WITH THE best team in the East would normally be a bright spot on Luol Deng's calendar, but he's feeling very glum. Eight days ago against the Grizzlies, he tore a ligament in his right wrist. Today the Bulls confirmed what he feared most: He'll have to undergo surgery on April 12. The news brings tears to his eyes.

"I didn't think my season would end like this," he says. "I hate not playing. I'm supposed to help this team win."

John Paxson calls Deng's injury a huge blow, especially after losing starting center Eddy Curry to an irregular heartbeat on March 30. But with Deng and his 11.7 points and 5.3 rebounds watching from the bench in a tan four-button suit, the Bulls press on toward their first post-season appearance in seven years.

Nobody expects great things from Jared Reiner. He is, after all, no Deng. Six months ago, the Bulls brought him into camp just to see what he could do. As a junior at the University of Iowa, he'd led the Big Ten Conference in rebounding. His professional highlights include a heads-up pass to guard Jannero Pargo and six overtime points in a preseason game. But tonight Reiner will help the Bulls forge a new history.

With Chicago trailing Miami by double figures, he steps onto the court with three fellow rookies—Andres Nocioni, Ben Gordon, and Chris Duhon, completing one of the greenest lineups the game has ever seen. This is a testament both to Scott Skiles' confidence in his young players and to their fearlessness in the face of NBA competition. Gordon makes a nice hustle play, stealing the ball and taking it the length of the court for a layup. Duhon rises up for a jumper, sees Nocioni gliding behind Rasual Butler, and passes him the ball for a quick inside hoop. They press up at halfcourt and throw their bodies about in the lane. They're scrappy, a complete embodiment of their coach. Their teamwork is no great leap for mankind, but it says more about the Bulls and where they're going than their 104–86 loss suggests.

With the win, the Heat lock up home-court advantage throughout the playoffs. This pleases Stan Van Gundy, who no longer has to worry about the prospect of playing four games in Detroit. But for the players, it's far less significant. "We're supposed to do that," says Damon Jones. "We're the best team in the East. Yeah, you have to take things one step at a time, but our goal is in June. It's that ring. We can't go patting ourselves on the back over this. Our job isn't done."

In the locker room after the game, I ask Keyon Dooling what he thinks about the Baby Bulls. "It's funny," he says. "With all that young talent, they kind of remind me of us a few years ago." By us, he means the 2000–01 Clippers. The connection between the two teams brings a smile to my face. I'm happy for Dooling. In one season with the Heat, he has logged more time on national television than he did in four seasons with the Clippers. After he tidies up his locker, he opens the overhead compartment, revealing several boxes of sneakers. He slides one out and puts it in my hands.

"Alright, Chris," he says. "I'll holla at you in a bit."

I need to touch base with Jones, but I don't want to send the wrong message—*Who let the klepto in?*—so I leave the box on the seat at Dooling's locker.

I linger around to chat with the trainers and beat writers. Turning to a guy from the *Palm Beach Post*, I say, "Give me a good Damon Jones story."

"There's a running joke around the team," he begins, "that Shaq is Shrek and Damon is Donkey."

My heart sinks. I'm well aware of the media's perception of Jones. The very same beat writers who love him for his motor mouth criticize him for his cockiness. I've learned not to expect too much from them. They're supposed to know everything there is to know about the teams they cover, but they rarely do.

I've got my own Damon Jones story from the day I first met him at Houston's Westside Tennis Club in 2002. He was lost in contemplation under a basket on the far side of the gym. I was listening to Steve Francis, Moochie Norris, and Rashard Lewis as they goofed around, pulling on their socks and lacing up their sneaks. The four men were a world apart that day. Francis, Norris, and Lewis had guaranteed contracts. Jones had nothing. So he approached every pick-up game that followed with mid-season focus. Cavaliers coach John Lucas organized these exhibitions a decade earlier and he carefully monitored them. He needed a point guard. Watching from the sideline, he reeled off a list of credentials. "I need somebody who can run all day," he said. "He's gotta be fast. My team is young and all they want to do is run, so I need someone to constantly push it. He's got to be able to throw the lob, too. Put it right up there for [then Cavalier] D-Miles. And I need someone who can do that for thirty minutes a game."

To Jones, this sounded like nirvana. "I'm looking to stick somewhere," he said. "It's all about years for me." And Lucas liked what he saw: Jones' speed, his leadership, and his willingness to shoulder the tough matchups, guys like Steve Francis who run you ragged. The coach invited Jones to training camp. But he continued to recruit candidates—former St. John's star Omar Cook and the well-traveled Rick Brunson—to see how well they meshed with his team. He also wined and dined Rod Strickland, hoping to woo the fourteen-year veteran to Cleveland's inexperienced roster with a $1 million offer.

The Cavs eventually traded for journeyman Milt Palacio, but, by showing up in the Westside gym every day, ready to play, Jones talked his way onto the Sacramento Kings' roster. When he was running his mouth, said Lucas, he had his head in the game.

Dooling is quick to confirm the coach's scouting report. "If Damon is talking, you know good things are happening," he says. "When he's quiet, something is definitely wrong."

And so, I politely withdraw from my conversation with the *Palm Beach Post* guy and hightail it to Dooling's locker to retrieve my shoes. A team trainer shoots me a dirty look.

"Keyon left these for me," I say, sheepishly. "Almost forgot 'em."

Next time through Miami, I'll bet I have someone shadowing me.

RACING ACROSS THE CAUSEWAY to South Beach, my spirits soar. I don't have to get up in the morning and deal with Miami International Airport. I'm going to drive north instead, catch the Bulls' next game in Orlando, before heading home to New York for a day or two. I roll all four windows down and let the warm air rush in.

I decide to stop for a pizza at old faithful: the Domino's on Alton Road between 14th Court and 14th Street. Cutting through the city's backstreets, I pull alongside the store, raising the windows. I'm on a first-name basis with the staff here. I can stick my head in the door and they pretty much know what I want.

"Medium pie, extra cheese," calls out the woman behind the counter.

"You got it," I reply. "Be back in a minute. I'm gonna run across the street and grab something to drink."

I page through the tabloids at 7-Eleven, searching for the latest on Jessica, Paris, and Lindsay while waiting for the foam to settle on my 64-ounce Double Gulp. *Ah, stars. They're just like us.* Beverage in hand, I cross the street feeling good. *The season's winding down. The book's working out. Got myself a new pair of shoes. Shoulda treated myself to pepperoni.*

As I approach my car, I notice the back windows. They're down. *Funny, I thought I'd rolled them up.* A few steps later, I spot a piece of paper on the ground. *The box score from tonight's game. The one that was handed to me in the locker room. Oh, shit.* I rush to the passenger's side, look in the rear window. The shoes Keyon gave me were on the seat…in plain view. They're gone. I had tucked the folded box score into my green and blue writers notebook, the very notebook in which I had scribbled down every quote, amusing anecdote, and noteworthy scene of the last few weeks. All the details from that day in Elton's studio. The notebook was in the shoebox.

Instinctively, I jog down the block. About fifty feet from the car, inches away from a giant puddle, I find my precious notebook and, a few paces later, the empty shoebox. I kick it into the bushes. How could I be so careless? Have I learned nothing from the computer meltdown? Why not just leave the car keys in the ignition?

On the bright side, it looks like I've dodged a bullet. I go inside to pick up my pizza. When I zip from the parking lot in my car, the Double Gulp is still on the roof.

ORLANDO, APRIL 6

I WAKE UP EARLY, drive two and a half hours to Orlando, and watch the Magic's morning shootaround, hoping to get a quote or two about the fallout from the Doug-Christie-for-Cuttino-Mobley trade with Sacramento. Sitting in the front seat of my Buick, I type up a story about how much Francis misses Mobley. When I'm finished, I use the towel I stole from the hotel to wipe the soda stains off the windshield.

LOS ANGELES, APRIL 7

ELTON BRAND IS A man of faith. He faithfully believes he can lift the Clippers into the playoffs. If not this year, then next. And how can he not? When you're in a dogfight, you must believe in your cause. When you're the Clippers team captain, you *really* must believe. But Brand's faith will not be rewarded this year.

After an 82–91 loss in San Antonio last night—the team's fifth defeat in seven games—the Clippers were officially eliminated from the post-season. "This team is getting closer," says Brand, already looking forward. "We're learning to do things in the clutch, down the stretch, that winning teams do. Plus we've got Shaun Livingston coming back full time next year and I believe that's going to make a big difference. There's no question that the playoffs are in our plans."

To be on the safe side, though, Brand has set some goals for the summer. After vacationing with Shahara and visiting friends and family back East, he'll look over the pictures in production at Gibraltar and drop by Hutton's studio to hear a track or two—no doubt taking Sunset to get there. But he plans to shed ten pounds too. He isn't overweight by any stretch, he just wants to quicken his step, to create a little more space on the floor for his jumpshot. That's how you keep the faith—by improving your game from one year to the next.

NEW YORK, APRIL 8

JEROME WILLIAMS OF THE Knicks sends Tyson Chandler soaring into the air with a pump fake. Floating helplessly above the court, the Bulls' fourth-year center hacks at Williams' wrist and argues the call with the ref. Scott Skiles subs Andres Nocioni while Chandler gets an earful from assistant coach Pete Myers.

"Stay on your feet," shouts Myers. "Shit!"

Chandler is caught off guard.

"Damn, Pete, what the fuck?"

The only open seat on the bench is next to Myers. Chandler goes to sit, but changes his mind, marching down the sideline and lowering himself onto a stack of towels. His knees shoot almost above his head. He has a look of pure frustration on his face.

"Don't be mad at me," Myers screams.

"I went straight up! Fuck!"

"Okay, you didn't foul him. There, does that make you feel better?"

Mumbling under his breath, dropping F-bombs like scuds, Chandler stares daggers into the floorboards, unfazed even when Knicks forward Michael Sweetney nearly crashes onto his head while chasing a loose ball out of bounds.

The game, though hard-fought, has deteriorated into a slopfest. Two fans in Madison Square Garden couldn't care less. Barely in their twenties, they've had their share of $8 beers and they're trying to get the attention of the Bulls' Jared Reiner, who's busy cheering his way through another DNP—Coach's Decision.

"We love you, Jared," calls out the Kelly Clarkson lookalike, baring more midriff than Reiner's got vertical leap.

"We want to meet you," screams her bleached-blonde sidekick. "Hey, Jared, over here."

"Anybody who drinks beer with a straw has mental problems," says former *Slam* editor Russ Bengtson, who's sitting to my right.

Reiner keeps his eyes on the Bulls' five-point lead as the clock dips below two minutes. But he's a rookie and these are hot chicks so he can't help but sneak a peek. He offers his new fan club a bit of a smile and they jump up and down screaming like schoolgirls.

Jared, you dog, you.

"Hey, Jared, you're a pimp!" shouts the guy behind me. "Iowa State rules!"

Yes, these are good times to be a Chicago Bull. After winning ten of their last eleven games, Skiles' team is closing in on the fifth seed in the East and they match up well with their likely opponent—the Washington Wizards. Luol Deng continues to travel with them, bum wrist and all. He can't bear to sit at home feeling sorry for himself, so he rallies his teammates from the wings, trying hard to force a smile. "It hurts not being able to play," he says, fighting not to choke up.

Long after the Knicks game concludes in a 102–94 victory for Chicago, Reiner's fanclub is hanging over the railing alongside the tunnel to the locker room. "Hey you," one of them calls to me. "Can you see what's taking Jerry Rider so long? He's supposed to come back out here and talk to us."

"You mean *Jared Reiner*?"

"Jared? Whatever. He was the tall, skinny, white guy who didn't play. He was looking at us all game. He wants to meet us."

"Hate to break it to you, sweetheart, but he's already on the bus."

"Can you check the locker room? Please. Pretty please."

"He liked us," chimes the second one. "He told us to wait right here. His name is Jeremy, he's the cute, skinny, white guy."

"Can you give him a note for us?" the first one says.

"You're going to be waiting a long time. He's gone."

Their shoulders slump and their mouths droop.

"Sorry," I say, even though I'm not. "By the way, what are you girls doing tonight?"

MIAMI, APRIL 10

TWO WEEKS AGO, THIS game loomed large. In Miami and Detroit, it was shaping up to be a preview of the Eastern Conference finals. But the Heat have cooled in their last two games thanks to a stomach virus that sidelined their jovial center. "No knock on them," says Rip Hamilton. "But we're supposed to win without Shaq."

Detroit holds Miami to a season-low 72 points.

No NBA star, not even LeBron James, has broken out the way Dwyane Wade has this season. But with four Detroit defenders swamping him, he's a totally different player. He can't get to the rim. With the lane effectively closed off, he should look to pass. Instead, he leans too heavily on his suspect jumpshot. He finishes with five points. "Just another day at the office," says Rasheed Wallace.

Clearly agitated, the ever-congenial Stan Van Gundy snaps at reporters after the game. He knows better than most that the success of the Heat hinges on Shaq's health. These days, that's a perilous proposition. Though still the best center in the league by a moonshot, Shaq doesn't frighten opponents as he once did. At 33, his window is closing. He's no longer the No. 1 option on offense. That role belongs to Wade. He can't battle for rebounds as he did in his Laker days.

After one leap, he's spent. And he can't shake the nagging little injuries as quickly. In fact, some people in the organization secretly wonder if Shaq will ever be 100 percent healthy again.

Van Gundy hates these hiccups in his plans and why shouldn't he? He's under enormous pressure. In the last two years, twenty-three of his peers have lost their jobs, including every head coach in what had been, before this season's realignment, the NBA's Atlantic Division. What's more, Van Gundy's leash is a good bit shorter than most, because Miami's front office has done such a terrific job of assembling a championship-caliber team. To save his head, Van Gundy has to win and win big…with Pat Riley watching from the shadows. As the team's president, the man who put all of those pieces together, Riley doesn't meddle in Van Gundy's business. In this, the Heat's best season ever, he's rarely quoted in the newspaper. He surfaces just long enough to make it known that he has no designs on Van Gundy's job. But Stan Van Gundy is a basketball coach and basketball coaches know not to get too comfortable. And Pat Riley is an ex-basketball coach and ex-basketball coaches never get the itch to coach out of their systems. Van Gundy is no fool. Neither is Riley.

LOS ANGELES, APRIL 15

WHEN SHAQ LIVED IN Los Angeles, he loved to get in the car at night and drive to clear his head. Game night or off night—it didn't matter. He'd grab the keys and go. Leave the sleeping kids behind. Tell his wife, Shaunie, not to wait up. He'd leave his 15,000-square-foot mansion in the hills of Mulholand Estates—Wayne Gretzky and Tom Arnold were neighbors—and head down leafy Beverly Glen to Sunset, where he'd turn left and drive by all the happening nightspots, peering out his window to see what was doing. From there he'd turn right onto La Cienega for a pitstop at Jerry's Deli. A sandwich or two later, he'd continue on La Cienega, hang a right on 3rd, pick up Wilshire by way of Santa Monica, then make one last right onto Beverly Glen and head home.

Tonight I feel like communing with Shaq.

I've gained thirteen pounds since the season started. I've slept in my own bed twice in twenty-four days. I haven't exercised one lick, unless dialing for takeout counts as physical activity. Not a week has gone by when I haven't eaten at Domino's, Carl's Jr., McDonald's or Boston Market. I'm just not taking care of myself.

A friend of mine keeps trying to get me to read a book about the dangers of a bad diet. I'm too afraid. The vintage T-shirts I bought with Miss Nikki on Melrose no longer fit. I'm not sure they ever did. I've tossed them aside for Richard Hamilton-approved XXXL shirts.

I do most of my writing between the hours of midnight and 6 a.m., and, by most, I mean all. Including the sentence you're reading right now. When I write, the adrenaline flows, my mind races. It doesn't stop until I've exhausted every last drop of energy. So, like Shaq, I get out the keys and bolt for the car. I like his route, but it's a bit out of the way when you're staying at the Marriott in Marina Del Rey. I start out on Washington Boulevard instead, driving east through Culver City. At Motor Avenue, I hang a left for a peaceful, curvy drive through the charming neighborhood of Cheviot Hills. I love the fact that Motor originates at the threshold of Sony Pictures Studios in Culver City and ends 2.7 miles later at the doorstep of 20th Century Fox Studios. *Look to your left at any point along the way and you're likely to see an idiot writer with nothing better to do.*

At 20th Century Fox, I turn left onto Pico and drive for three blocks before making a right onto Beverly Glen, skirting 90210, before making a left onto Sunset in the hills behind UCLA. I follow that route for maybe ten miles to the Pacific Coast Highway, steering the car south to my hotel. Before calling it a night, I stop for a Famous Star combo at the 24-hour Carl's Jr. on Sepulveda.

Shaq gained thirty pounds in L.A. Maybe I'm lucky.

SOMEHWERE, OH YEAH, MIAMI, NO WAIT, DALLAS, APRIL 23

THIS IS A JOURNEY of self-discovery. That's what I keep telling people.

"Well, what have you discovered about yourself?"

That's the dreaded follow-up. I've become quite adept at dodging it.

"Hey, look over there!" I yell, before running full speed in the other direction. Works every time. Just so long as I don't bump into anyone with a better time in the 40.

I'm at a bit of a loss for words. I've taken more than seventy flights, rented twenty-two cars, driven almost 3,000 miles, ordered seventeen pizzas, stolen (roughly) twelve hotel towels, recorded hundreds of hours of interviews, scribbled countless notes and lost one tooth, which will never grow back the way they do in cartoons. I've watched sixty games in twenty-two arenas and aged several months in each of the country's time zones. I'm struck by how fast it all flew by.

Have you ever seen that movie trick where the main character stands on a busy city block and the world around him speeds past in fast forward. That's how I feel. The flights, the games, the players, the words—everything is mashed together. I can't remember the conversation I had with Tracy McGrady two days ago, but this curious image from four months back is etched on my brain: Dwyane Wade, fully dressed, leaving the United Center locker room with his left shoe untied. I can barely make sense of it all. I'm watching a game at the

AmericanAirlines Arena in Miami and I step through an exit and suddenly I'm in the parking lot of The Palace of Auburn Hills. McGrady is sitting next to me on a flight from L.A. to Chicago. Mike Dunleavy is coaching the Wizards. Kobe Bryant is working the drive-thru at Carl's Jr.

I open my laptop and find myself looking into another dimension. I'm afraid to place my hands on the keyboard for fear I might get sucked into a black hole. Yes, self-discovery is tiring. You can't have a life when you work on a book like this. Well, you can, but it's not a real one. It's someone else's. Nights in VIP rooms, pretending I like champagne. Riding around in Bentleys that don't belong to me. Chatting up wannabe models who are out of my league and are only talking to me because I can introduce them to an athlete who's wearing a watch that would set me back two years' salary.

When someone asks me to hang out on a game night, I hit him with an odd response: "I can't. I have to go to a game tonight."

I *have* to go to a game. I *have* to go to a game?

Over the course of five months, *get to go* has somehow morphed into *have to go*. Maybe it's age. Maybe it's because I've peeked behind the curtain and seen the strings. Whatever the reason, I no longer revere professional basketball players.

"Get it out of your system," my friend Scoop told me.

Don't worry. I'm not asking you to feel sorry for me. It doesn't take a whole lot of self-discovery to remember why I'm here. Not to write a book, but for the same reason I used to get up at 6 a.m. to shoot jumpshots.

Basketball.

At the heart of it all is my love for the game.

And, hey, look at that: The playoffs start today!

THE PLAYOFFS: FIRST ROUND

EASTERN CONFERENCE

WESTERN CONFERENCE

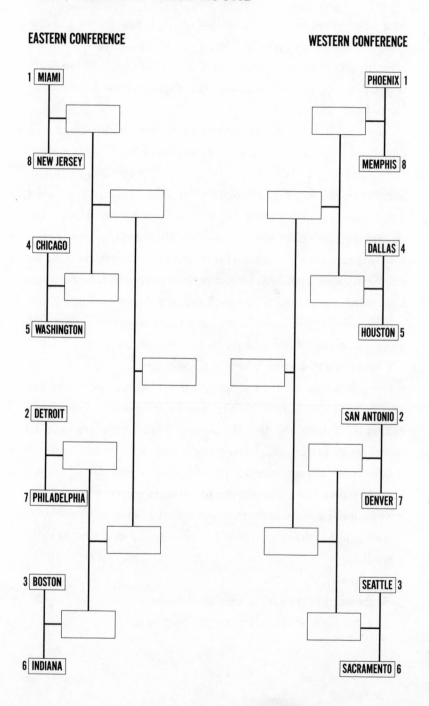

A SAD DAY IN DALLAS

DALLAS, APRIL 25

YOU KNOW WHAT'S IMPORTANT about the playoffs? The little things. Boxing out. Running your lane. Clapping for teammates when they miss their free throws. The stuff that goes unnoticed when you don't have someone like me to point it out. Where better to find that stuff than in the first-round matchup between the Mavericks and the Rockets?

T-Mac will hate me for saying this, but I hope the Mavericks don't get swept. Not because I love to watch their amazing talent and not because I don't want to see them punctuate another outstanding season with an early exit, but because American Airlines Center in Dallas is the most exciting place to watch an NBA game. The city is crawling with knowledgeable fans. Note the I LOVE JOSH HOWARD sign. The people here are punctual, too. After witnessing a 98–86 train wreck in Game One, a record crowd of 20,884 has convened twenty minutes before tip-off to set the record straight.

Reaching back to the Eighties, the home team charges onto the court to the strains of Kool Moe Dee's "I Go to Work." That's the little stuff I'm talking about. Jason Terry sits on the cushioned scorer's table, massaging his left hamstring. He reaches for a bottle of chalk, the kind M.J. made cool by playfully clapping it into clouds in the faces of the Bulls radio guys. Nowadays, lots of players copy the move. Not Terry. He gently shakes the powder from the bottle, spits in his right palm, rubs his hands together and wipes the bottoms of his shoes. The Mavericks' radio guys must feel left out. Then again, Terry is a wee bit odd. Lately, he's been wearing Rockets practice shorts to bed. He wears three new pairs of knee-high socks to each game, throwing them in the trash immediately afterward. "They go to the sock graveyard," he says. If you're keeping score at home, that's nearly 500 casualties this season.

Mark Cuban, the owner of the Mavericks, passes behind me, tweaking my ear with his finger. He's the only guy I let do that. "What's up, Chris?" he says. Out on the court, every Dallas player is standing at attention, right hand over his heart, for the playing of the national anthem. Even Germany's Dirk Nowitzki. A handful of the guys even mouth the words. I make a note to e-mail Cuban and ask him if this is team policy. I've never seen such patriotism in the NBA.

Houston's players rock from side to side, hands folded behind their backs or tucked into the waistbands of their warm-ups. Nothing inappropriate, mind you. That's precisely what I'm doing (without the warm-ups, of course). That is, until the Mavs Dancers make their entrance, rushing onto the court in skintight outfits. The ladies get points for beauty and choreography, but they really shine in the style department. The rhinestone-studded G-strings that peak out a good two inches above their black leather low riders give the evening a Sin City feel.

But, hey, I'm here to watch basketball, and, as you might expect, the tempo in Dallas is fast and furious. The refs are working over-time, calling a foul a minute, but the fireworks are brilliant. The rims are mic'd, sending a jolt of lightning through the P.A. system every time a jump shot pops the chords. You can hear the players' grunts and growls, even an expletive or two.

McGrady leaps clear over Shawn Bradley for a dunk that brings down the house. The Mavs rain fire from the three-point line. My head's swiveling back and forth like the chair umpire at Wimbledon. I need a T.O.

Jeff Van Gundy is a firm believer in pound-it-in, half-court basketball, but he's smart enough to let this Rockets team run. Dallas' Keith Van Horn picks up three fouls in the first quarter and he isn't even a starter. That's gotta be a record. During the next timeout, the arena's DJ cues up the Foo Fighters' "Learn to Fly." *Run and tell all of the angels this could take all night,* sings frontman Dave Grohl. He's not kidding.

The Rockets lead 60–56 at the half. Inside the tunnel leading to the Dallas locker room, I spot a kid in a Nowitzki jersey and hand him my Mavs media guide. Now I know what Mean Joe Green feels like.

With the score tied in the fourth quarter and the final seconds ticking off the clock, McGrady's Rockets part with conventional wisdom. Instead of calling timeout, they inbound the ball, catching the backpedaling Mavericks off guard. With two ticks left, T-Mac calmly pushes the ball the length of the court and drills a pull-up jumper from twenty feet out to give his team a 113–111 victory. It's the kind of clutch play you expect from a championship player.

Spirits crushed, the Mavericks slink off the floor. In the post-game press conference, a reporter asks Dallas coach Avery Johnson why he didn't make more use of underrated swing guard Marquis Daniels.

"This is the playoffs," the coach replies. "Have you ever been to a playoff game?"

"I think so," says the reporter, a little slow off the dribble.

"Then you know rotations get shorter in the playoffs. Everybody can't play."

The locker room might as well be a tomb. "We're just in shock," says Nowitzki.

On a placard above the big screen TV against one wall, there's a quote from Coach Johnson. Don Nelson posted it there at the beginning of the season when Johnson was his assistant. It reads: "Contested shots will wound us. Uncontested shots and layups will kill us."

It's the little things that count, always the little things.

MIAMI, MAY 3

THE HEAT EARNED SOMETHING they've wanted for awhile, something simple but invaluable—rest. Two days ago, behind Dwyane Wade's 34-point outburst in the Meadowlands, they swept the New Jersey Nets from the post-season. Now they're waiting on the Bulls and the Wizards to decide their next opponent.

Coaches hate downtime like this. It messes with their team's rhythm. They insist on practicing to fight the rust that's quick to grow on NBA players. But Stan Van Gundy is not your average coach. He's generous with vacation days. His Heat limped into the playoffs and they'll be hard pressed to reach the Finals if they don't tend to their injuries. Shaq's undergoing daily treatment for thigh bruises, one inflicted by the Pacers on April 17, the other by the Nets two nights ago. Damon Jones is hobbled by a sprained left ankle. Doctors have advised him to secure it in a protective boot twenty hours a day.

There's not much that can dampen D.J.'s spirit though. He set an NBA record in the Nets series with 17 three-pointers in four games.

Reggie Miller and Derek Fisher owned the old mark of 15. Never has Jones played a more crucial role in his team's success. From behind the arc, he lit up the scoreboard on one out of every two shots.

But my man got even more attention for what he did off the court. Despite admonitions from the league's front office, he appeared on TV for a Game One press conference wearing a $400 pair of white-rimmed Yves Saint Laurent sunglasses. NBA Commissioner David Stern protested that the pricey shades prevented Jones from communing with the nationwide audience. "That's just ridiculous," Jones replied. "Who's more intimate than me? I've always been the type of player that people can touch."

Truth be told, he wasn't all that bothered by the scuffle. He loves the attention. Those sunglasses were the talk of sports radio. Tony Kornheiser and Michael Wilbon debated them on *Pardon the Interruption*. *ESPN The Magazine* dispatched a photographer to catch them on film. Today.

The moment I arrive on the sun-soaked beach for the shoot, I spot Christian Lantry, who photographed Sebastian Telfair in Coney Island for a story I wrote a year ago. Two months later, Telfair declared for the draft, becoming the shortest prep player in history to make the jump to the pros. I like visiting Christian's shoots. He's got an easy rapport with people.

After thirty minutes, Jones' silver Bentley appears on the sand. David Holcombe, the Heat's longtime director of security, emerges from the passenger seat—all 6-foot-3 hulking inches of him. I introduce myself. He looks me over with wary eyes. His handshake is ironclad. No up or down. Just a brief grasp. "David Holcombe, security," he says without a trace of warmth.

Like all photographers, Lantry is fixated on light. He wants to get Jones out on the beach right away. A beautiful Brazilian woman in her mid-thirties saunters up to Jones and politely instructs him to follow her into the RV that doubles as a make-up trailer. She guides him to his seat and immediately sets to work. I grab a handful of cashews and make small talk.

As you may recall, Jones bet Shaq that the Eagles would beat the Patriots in the Super Bowl. "Did you pay up?" I ask.

"I always pay up," he says. "You're not a man if you don't pay up."

The conversation halts right there.

"Did you bring your glasses with you?" Lantry interrupts.

"I never go anywhere without them," says Jones. He reaches for his designer handbag, unzipping it to reveal four pairs of beloved Yves Saint Laurents.

Lantry explains that he wants to shoot up close. He's hired extras to simulate Jones' fans. They include several teenaged girls, an elderly couple, two bikini-clad models and a 12-year-old boy with bushy hair. The shoot will place Jones in the position of thumbing his nose at the league. He doesn't seem to care. As we return to the sand, he's in awe of the fuss.

"Man, ESPN, girls in bikinis, I must be doing something right, wouldn't you say?"

Lantry commands the extras to jump up and down, screaming and cheering, behind Jones. "Louder," he shouts, snapping pictures. "Let's see some more energy!"

I step aside and try to chat up the steely Holcombe, who's miffed by the music pumping from the portable speakers of Lantry's iPod.

"No cuss words," he says. "If a song has cuss words, I don't want to hear it today. We got too many young people on set."

"Juicy" by Biggie Smalls vibes through the air.

"Is there any language in this song?" he asks.

"Ah, not to my knowledge," I lie. I'm tired of having him bust up the groove. To loosen up his shaved head, I ask him about Jones.

"He's cool, huh?"

"He's one of the best guys we've got around," Holcombe says.

"Yeah, cool guy. We had a great photo shoot with D. Wade back in September, too."

Holcombe shoots me an elbow to the ribs. It actually hurts.

"Yeah, we didn't really like that one too much," he says.

We?

In October, I wrote a magazine feature heralding Wade as the next big thing. The photo editor arranged for a high-profile shoot on the rooftop of a trendy South Beach hotel. Wade posed poolside, holding a martini, surrounded by a bevy of microbikini-wearing models. He wore a black jacket with his tie undone. In the next shot, he was dancing with his lovely harem, dressed to kill for a night on the town. The tie was gone. A Miami Heat dancer, a stunning, 5-foot-10 blonde with fake breasts, was told to flirt with him as if she were at a party. She put her pink glossy lips up to Wade's right ear and whispered something I'd give a week's pay to hear. The picture didn't exactly match Wade's clean-cut image, but he was more than happy to comply. "This is the life," he said.

Jones seems to be enjoying himself, too—despite the prying eyes of his chaperone. He flashes a great big smile from behind the wheel of his Bentley as Lantry spools through his last roll of film. Those overnight van rides in the CBA are a thing of the past now, something to laugh about. Damon Jones never has to set foot in Black Hills, South Dakota, again.

DETROIT, MAY 6

RICHARD HAMILTON PARKS HIS narrow butt in a black swivel chair, the kind you find in the offices of CEOs, and shifts his weight until he feels comfortable.

"Just look straight?" he asks.

"Straight ahead into the camera," replies the producer. "It'll feel kind of funny, but it'll be fine."

Five hundred miles away in Times Square, John Saunders, host of ESPN's *NBA Shootaround*, is doing the exact same thing. After eliminating the Philadelphia 76ers in five games, the Pistons are bracing for a tough test of wills in their second-round match-up with Indiana. With his first question, Saunders zeroes in on the two teams' infamous brawl.

"How have you guys responded since the November 19 incident in Detroit? Is it something you still think about?"

The Pistons have, for the most part, put the whole thing behind them. The beat reporters in Detroit barely broach the subject anymore. Their new obsession is peripatetic Larry Brown, who's flirting with jetting to New York to coach the Knicks. But a nationally televised interview must include a question or two about the fight. Rip knows that.

"At first it took awhile for us to get back into the swing of things," he says. "It definitely had our minds in a funk and was one of the reasons we started off the way we did. But it was the suspensions from the fight that hurt us more than anything. Ben was out and we were missing something without him."

Without Wallace patrolling the paint, LeBron James lit up Detroit in November for 43 points, penetrating the defense for layups and dunks almost at will. "He could have gotten 60 that night," said Larry Brown.

"I think the whole thing has been erased from peoples' minds," Rip says now. "I know it has been from ours. Really, I don't even think about it. As a team, we've all moved on."

DALLAS, MAY 7

IT'S AN HOUR BEFORE Game Seven of the Rockets-Mavericks series and TNT sideline reporter David Aldridge is talking with Fort Worth *Star-Telegram* columnist Dwain Price and Rockets PR man Nelson Luis outside the Houston locker room. One of the big guns on the NBA beat, Aldridge has always been generous with career advice. "It's quiet in there," he says, motioning toward the door. I push it open and step inside.

Normally, when you walk into a pre-game locker room, the players glance up—at least momentarily—before turning away hoping that you'll leave them alone. No one here moves a muscle. The stillness is almost eerie. In the far right corner of the room, Tracy McGrady sits staring at a TV replaying the Rockets 101–83 Game Six victory. Opposite him, peering blankly from his metal folding chair, is Yao Ming. Backup point guard Mike James stretches in the middle of the floor. Jon Barry has to step over him on the way to his locker. The sole sign of life is the pulsating light on the front of Moochie Norris's seventeen-inch PowerBook.

McGrady stands up and pads across the carpet. We shake hands.

"You ready for this?" I ask.

"Most definitely," he replies, "As ready as I'll ever be. Somebody has to go home tonight."

Eight seasons into his NBA career, McGrady has never advanced to the second round of the playoffs. In 2003, he steered the Orlando Magic to a three-games-to-one lead over Detroit, then endured three straight losses by an average of 20 points. "We didn't have enough to close it out," he said at the time. But this Rockets team has plenty of firepower. Six games into the series, they lead the Mavericks in shooting percentage, defensive rebounds, assists and blocked shots. This Game Seven is one they can win. For McGrady, it's a must-win.

The home-court crowd is pulling hard for Dallas. A woman in the front row holds a sign with a cartoon depicting Dirk Nowitzki kicking T-Mac in the behind. The four teenagers behind me have giant letters painted on their naked chests. Together they spell V-A-M-S. One rings a cowbell he stole from a hardware store. "I'll bring it back when the Mavs get eliminated," he says. Another holds a length of plastic PVC pipe. Each time he blows into it, he leaves a circle imprinted in the blue face paint around his mouth.

Forty-eight seconds into the game, Yao picks up his first foul. His confidence is shot. In Game Two, he led all Rockets scorers with 33 points. He spent the fourth quarter of Game Six on the bench. McGrady's hopes are fading fast. Leading 16–14 midway through the first quarter, the Mavericks explode on a 33–11 run. T-Mac can't seem to find his shot. With 6:42 left in the half, he draws a technical foul for voicing his displeasure with the officiating.

The second half brings him more heartache. Despite 27 points, seven assists and seven rebounds, McGrady is powerless to change the outcome. The final score—116–76—goes into the record books as the biggest Game Seven whipping in NBA history.

"I'm still dizzy. They hit us hard," says Norris in the somber post-game locker room. "Game Seven was like a title fight and we got knocked out."

McGrady is the first player dressed. He stands and shuffles past me, head down, eyes to the floor. I know enough to stay out of his way. I watch him duck into the trainer's room, where a team official is pulling the tape from Dikembe Mutombo's ankles. Juwan Howard sits facing the back of his chair, fully dressed, his chin resting on his arms. It looks as if someone just told him he had to report to summer school.

Rockets coach Jeff Van Gundy greets the press with the ever-present can of Diet Coke in his right hand. He sits down and clears his throat. "We cracked," he says. "That's what happened to us tonight. In the biggest game of the year, we just cracked under the weight. We cracked in every way."

The Rockets took horrible shots. They didn't get back on D. They played with all the energy of a slug tanning its back on a sunny afternoon.

As coaches often do, Van Gundy tips his hat to the opposition. But the sentiment rings hollow. It's not in his makeup to praise the heart of an opponent, not when his whole coaching philosophy is built on effort. In a cruel twist of fate, he finds himself applauding Avery Johnson, the man who drilled an eighteen-footer on the left baseline in Game Five of the 1999 Finals to eliminate Van Gundy's Knicks. Six years later, as head coach of the Mavericks, he's stuck it to Van Gundy again.

McGrady sinks into a folding chair and adjusts the mic, not because it's out of place, but because this is what players do to shed nervous energy. He pauses. Exhales. Not one peep from the assembled press corps. No one dares to ask a question. We simply wait for McGrady to start talking. "I am…I am…I'm disgusted," he says, struggling with the words. "I'm really mad and angry. All that stuff. This wasn't us tonight. That's not what we worked all this time for. But, at the same time, I'm already thinking about next season and how I'm going to come out."

Classic McGrady: He sees the play unfolding, the whispers that will dog him all summer long. *He can't win when it counts. He should never have left Vince Carter in Toronto. He was the source of all that turmoil in Orlando. John Weisbrod was right—Tracy McGrady is the problem. He's a Dominique Wilkins in the making. A Stephon Marbury.*

McGrady sees the play and responds. "I'm very disappointed, but I'm not going to hang my head. I'm 25 years old and I've got a lot of years left in this league. All this that I'm going through is only going to make me tougher. I'll never fold. Not even if I get bounced out of the first round three more times. I'm too tough for that."

He's happy to play the bad guy. He likes the challenge of proving people wrong.

He pushes back his chair, stands, and heads for the door. I meet him halfway.

"Are you going to watch the rest of the playoffs?" I ask.

"Without a doubt," he says. "I'm still a fan. I'm always going to be a fan."

And with that, his season draws to a close. I shake his hand and wish him well. He walks down the hall and turns the corner out of sight.

THE CONFERENCE SEMIFINALS

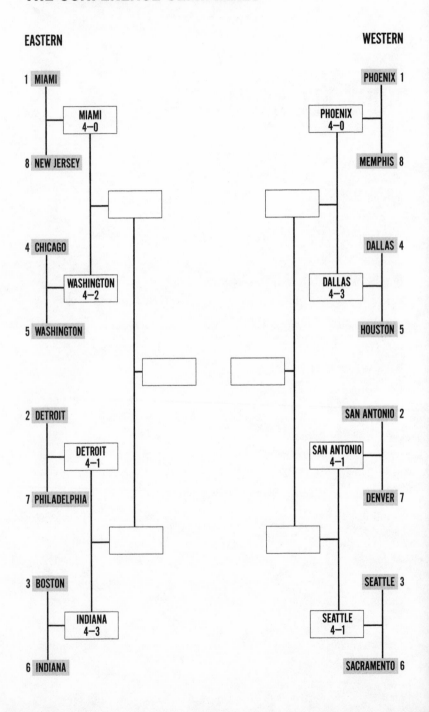

EASTERN

WESTERN

1 MIAMI

MIAMI
4–0

8 NEW JERSEY

4 CHICAGO

WASHINGTON
4–2

5 WASHINGTON

2 DETROIT

DETROIT
4–1

7 PHILADELPHIA

3 BOSTON

INDIANA
4–3

6 INDIANA

PHOENIX 1

PHOENIX
4–0

MEMPHIS 8

DALLAS 4

DALLAS
4–3

HOUSTON 5

SAN ANTONIO 2

SAN ANTONIO
4–1

DENVER 7

SEATTLE 3

SEATTLE
4–1

SACRAMENTO 6

HUGS ALL AROUND

MIAMI, MAY 8

"YOU DON'T STOP SHAQ," says Wizards point guard Gilbert Arenas, sitting in AmericanAirlines Arena's bare-bones visitors' locker room. "No one stops Shaq. No one's ever stopped Shaq."

No disrespect to Jared Jeffries, Brendan Haywood, or Etan Thomas, but that's just the way it is. The Wizards may have reached the play-offs for the first time since 1997, even advanced to the second round with a dogfight of a Game Six win versus the equally-inspired Bulls, but their overachieving front line doesn't cut it—not against a 7-foot-1, 325-pound freak of nature. The best they can hope for is to steal a game.

Not tonight, though. Dwyane Wade shoots a paltry 2-of-9 from the floor in the first half and Shaq gets himself into foul trouble, and still the Heat pile up an 18-point lead behind the hot hand of Keyon Dooling. Alonzo Mourning chips in the highlight of the game. Late in the first quarter, after a broken play at halfcourt, he chases down Arenas, swooping in like some great big raptor to foil his dunk. Arenas promptly retreats to the Wizards locker room to change his shorts. The first pair felt too restrictive, he says.

The Heat win 105–86, but you wouldn't know it to look at the faces in the locker room. Miami's towering expectations are beginning to take their toll. I blame Stan Van Gundy. Any time a team wins by 19 and the players start critiquing their play, you can bet it's the coach doing the talking. Players don't think that way. And with good reason: They can survive for eons on an awful team; coaches get the boot after one rough stretch. Two weeks ago, Van Gundy put the finishing touches on one of the best seasons in franchise history. Tonight, that's old news.

MIAMI, MAY 9

I WAKE UP TODAY to some news that blows my wig back: LeBron James has fired Aaron Goodwin. *Woah, nobody saw this coming. Not the media, not the Cavs, not Goodwin himself.* "I'm stunned by everything that is happening," he tells my colleague Darren Rovell of ESPN.com. "We did everything for LeBron to help mold him off the court and become the next big icon in sports. If what we did over the past two years led him to believe that he no longer needs an agent, then I guess we didn't do too bad."

Not too bad indeed. LeBron's annual endorsement income ranks No. 4 in the world, behind that of Tiger Woods, Michael Schumacher and David Beckham. And did I mention that he's all of 20 years old?

LeBron says he plans to place his career in the hands of his Four Horsemen friends. Maverick Carter, a consultant for Nike, will serve as lead negotiator; Randy Mims will act as manager; and Richard Paul will be a paid consultant.

I call Paul, who's listed as Shorty on my speed dial, to get the scoop.

"Bron just wants to show he hasn't forgotten where he's from," he says. "As the Four Horsemen, we're in this together. People think we're just living off him, but we'll show everybody how we function as a team. Bron relies on us and it's our job to be there for him."

He closes by saying that the Horsemen are poised to take LeBron to "a level that no other athlete has gone before."

I wish him luck, feeling fortunate to be cool with the new crew. Maybe LeBron will come back to *The Magazine*. For a split second, I think that Goodwin got what he deserves, but I don't really believe that. This is just the way the NBA works. One day you're negotiating $100 million deals, the next you're out on your ass.

Besides there's no reason to feel sorry for the guy. He still gets a cut of LeBron's income from every deal he negotiated. And, hey, I don't bear him any ill will.

My Motorola Razr begins ringing again the moment I slap it shut. With nothing on my to-do list, I had planned to sleep late into the afternoon, but ESPN producer Matt Wilansky wants me to tape a promo for *Top 5 Reasons You Can't Blame Jerry Krause for the Demise of the Bulls*, a new show on ESPN2. "You gotta be at the studio in an hour," he says. Here's the catch. I'll be debating *Chicago Sun-Times* columnist Jay Mariotti on the former GM's record. Mariotti gets paid to argue with people on television. I do not, and I'm completely unprepared. This could get ugly.

I jot down some notes on hotel stationary, do a half-ass ironing job on my purple pinstriped shirt, and fly out the door. I swerve onto I-95, wiping the sleep from my eyes. The hotel stationary sails out the window. Looks like I'm going to have to wing it.

WASHINGTON, D.C., MAY 12

IN 1986, I SAW my first NBA game at the Capital Centre in Landover, Maryland. My mother drove me to the arena in our old Ford Grenada. We never knew if and when its engine was going to quit. Every stoplight heightened the suspense. As I bolted through the Capital Centre doors, walked to the edge of the concourse, and peered out onto the court, I was struck by how vivid the action looked. TV didn't do it justice. I was amazed to hear the bouncing of the ball. From where we sat, about thirty rows up, it made a muffled tap, tap, tap as if the dark brown globe the pros were using was wrapped in soft leather. My hands tingled with the desire to touch it. I'd never held a ball like that. I was used to the rubber ones you use on playgrounds, the kind that ping when you bounce them.

The crowd was quiet. When Michael Jordan swooped to the goal and eased an incredible reverse layup past the outstretched arms of Manute Bol, there was a faint buzz. Beyond that, just the steady hum of people shuffling in their seats. The Cap Centre did not resemble a sports venue so much as an airplane hangar.

The Bullets had a theme song in those days. The chorus was, "That's the reason I'm a Bullets fan." No one took it to heart. The Capitals and Redskins had legions of loyal supporters. The Bullets had observers.

But much has changed in the last decade—including the team nickname. Citing the franchise's ties to a city with one of the nation's highest murder rates, owner Abe Pollin dispensed with the old tag in 1997. He neglected to mention that his Bullets were dead last in merchandise sales. The new nickname was immediately condemned by people who noted the Ku Klux Klan's fondness for Wizards.

Today, Washington plays in the sparkling MCI Center in D.C.'s revitalized downtown. The team has a promising young roster and fans intoxicated by the style of play. On the night of Game Three versus the Heat, the atmosphere inside the arena is electric. The crowd is younger than I recall: cable TV-raised sport-a-holics who love nothing more than to scream, scream, scream for the home team. African Americans sit closer to the court here than in most cities, a sign of Washington's upwardly mobile middle class. Rising to their feet, they cheer and wave towels, unfazed by the very real prospect that the overmatched Wizards will soon be swept aside. With the Skins, the Caps, the recent arrival Nationals, and Pollin's revamped NBA franchise, D.C. is once again a sports town, and, if sports towns are about one thing, it's hope. The hope that next year will be better. That Johnny's ankle will heel in time for football season. That the high fly ball stays inside the foul pole. That the 18–12 Richmond Spiders crash the NCAA Tournament and topple top-seeded Duke. No dream in sports is too grand.

If only the world weren't such a heartless place. After the inevitable 102–95 Heat triumph, Alonzo Mourning struts from the visitors' locker room, clad in an impeccable suit, and a small television monitor catches his eye. There on the screen is a younger version of himself, dressed in a Georgetown uniform, swatting away shot after shot. He pauses, transfixed, his now grizzled face brightened by a sentimental grin. "Man, that takes me back," he says, voice cracking. "Coach Thompson really taught me a lot."

The grin blossoms into a full-blown smile.

"And I was pretty slim back then, too. Man, look at me go."

In Washington, D.C., Zo has good reason to smile. Everywhere he goes, people stop him to talk G-Town. "The four years I spent here were some of the best of my life," he says. "We should have won it all in '89."

I remember that team. I lived that team. Saw every one of its games on television. I worshipped Zo; used to pretend I was point guard Charles Smith. At a Bulls-Bullets game in 1989, I came face to face with the guys whose photographs papered the walls in my room. At halftime, on the concourse level of the Capital Centre, both signed my ticket stub. I still have it. Two years later, Smith struck and killed two young women with his car. Instead of scaling the NBA's heights, he went to prison.

WASHINGTON, D.C., MAY 14

WHEN DAMON JONES FINDS himself in the spotlight, when a question, *any question*, no matter how routine, is posed, he loves to wax poetic. His voice softens, rising in time to the drama of the story he's telling. He uses pauses to great effect. If nothing else, the man's a performer. He covets the podium. And you can't fault him for that. He waited a lifetime for this moment. And his faith and his hard work are finally paying off. With Shaq watching from the sideline, the Heat advance to the Eastern Conference finals, making quick work of the Wizards in Game Four. O'Neal's tortured thighs will get yet more rest before they have to face the biggest challenge of the season—a looming showdown with the Detroit Pistons. For Jones, this is a good time to reflect. And, as it so happens, he's sitting behind a microphone with an audience in front of him.

"Can you really sum up how this feels?" I ask him.

He reaches for the mic. Pulls it closer to his mouth.

"This to me is…it's something I've waited for. Coming from where I did, not knowing whether or not I'd have a job the next morning, the ten-day contracts, constantly getting traded…all this right now is payback for all the hard work I've put in. I want to just cherish this for a minute."

He leans back in his chair, beyond the microphone's reach, shakes his head and whispers to himself, "Eastern Conference finals, man."

Shortly after midnight, a pearl green Range Rover noses up to the players' exit in the Wizards parking garage. The guard waves the vehicle through, but the driver pumps the brakes instead. His tinted black window descends to reveal the beaming mug of Gilbert Arenas. "We got a lot to smile about," he says as a cluster of fans uncap their Sharpies.

Yes, his team was swept. But all of D.C. is abuzz with pride. "This is an exciting time," says head coach Eddie Jordan. "What a wonderful learning experience. We've got great coaches, dedicated players, and one tremendous fan base. And we've got our leader, Gilbert. Going forward things are only going to get better."

For once, a Wizards coach speaks the truth.

INDIANAPOLIS, MAY 19

SIX MONTHS TO THE date of their nasty brawl, the Pistons stand clapping as Indiana's Reggie Miller walks to the bench in tears. Fifteen seconds away from a trip to the Eastern Conference finals, coach Larry Brown calls timeout to extend the ovation. One by one, Miller hugs Detroit's players. When he gets to Richard Hamilton, he pauses for an exchange of words.

"Thank you for everything you've done," Hamilton says. "I've always appreciated the way you played the game."

"Hey, listen, just continue to carry the torch," Miller replies. "You're doing it the right way."

Hamilton has 28 points, Miller 27.

The Pacers legend had decided Game Two eight nights earlier with one of his memorable clutch performances—scoring 15 of his 19 points in the second half as the Pacers rallied to tie the series. Riding on his 39-year-old legs against Detroit's withering defense, he tried to summon the magic once more in Game Six tonight, hitting a three-pointer with under two minutes left to pull Indiana within three, 82–79. But Hamilton responded with a jumper and Detroit held firm for an 88–79 win, ending Miller's eighteen-year quest for a championship ring.

The last of the great superstars drafted in the Eighties, Miller the leaves the court as the No. 12 scorer in NBA history with 25,279 points. Hamilton is appropriately awed by the comparisons between the two players—their rail-thin bodies, their outsized hearts, their sniper-like games.

"It was an honor for me to have played against him," says Rip. "He's always played the game the way it's supposed to be played and I've always respected him for that. He's definitely one of the all-time greats."

The league now belongs to the next generation of stars and its resiliency is never more apparent than on this night. "How about that?" Larry Brown says. "We played three games since the fight, six games in the playoffs, and guys were hugging each other."

THE CONFERENCE FINALS

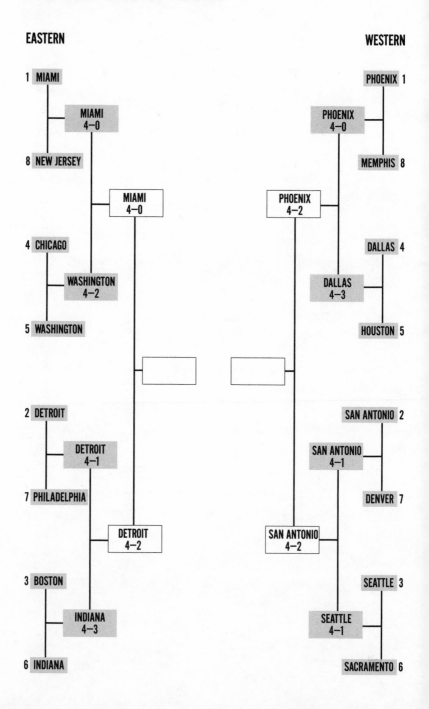

EASTERN

WESTERN

1 MIAMI

MIAMI
4–0

8 NEW JERSEY

MIAMI
4–0

4 CHICAGO

WASHINGTON
4–2

5 WASHINGTON

2 DETROIT

DETROIT
4–1

7 PHILADELPHIA

DETROIT
4–2

3 BOSTON

INDIANA
4–3

6 INDIANA

PHOENIX 1

PHOENIX
4–0

MEMPHIS 8

PHOENIX
4–2

DALLAS 4

DALLAS
4–3

HOUSTON 5

SAN ANTONIO 2

SAN ANTONIO
4–1

DENVER 7

SAN ANTONIO
4–2

SEATTLE 3

SEATTLE
4–1

SACRAMENTO 6

HANNIBAL AND THE GLADIATORS

MIAMI, MAY 23

I LOVE IT WHEN *a plan comes together.*

That was the catch phrase of Hannibal, played by George Peppard on *The A-Team*, one of the few programs on TV that could pull me away from basketball when I was a kid. I find myself repeating those words today.

Back in December, when I was cursing Aaron Goodwin and Jamal Crawford, sweating over Baron Davis and Dwight Howard, I couldn't foresee how things would unfold. Had all those players cooperated, my story would have ended in April when the Knicks, the Warriors, and the Magic bowed out of the playoff race. Instead, I've got two players gunning for the NBA Finals.

I'll never question the basketball gods again.

According to team rules, Miami's players must arrive at AmericanAirlines Arena two hours before tip off, but tonight they begin trickling in the door an hour early. Each finds a thick blue sheet of paper at his locker. Printed in red ink in the upper right hand corner of the page is the recipient's name. Across the top: Detroit Personnel. Below: a detailed scouting report for every player on the Pistons, compiled by the Heat coaches and scouts after viewing hundreds of hours of game film. If a member of the Pistons has so much as sneezed in the last six months, Miami knows about it. Detroit forward Darvin Ham, famous for once shattering a backboard in the NCAA basketball tournament, has played a grand total of ten minutes in the post-season. The Heat critiqued them: "explosive leaper, lob threat! (after to), only 3 fgm outside 2', vg offensive reb'nder." [Translation: great leaper, lob threat (after a turnover), only three field goals made more than two feet beyond the basket, very good offensive rebounder.] The book on Rasheed Wallace: "trails for open 3's...spins out right for lobs...[can go] both ways on rare drive."

Damon Jones skips over both players. The Pistons he may be called upon to guard are underlined in red ink. Carlos Arroyo will no doubt take umbrage to being labeled a "slow footed, poor defender...[who] flops," but that's how Miami's staff sizes him up. Jones doesn't waste time committing that to memory, though. He's consumed with guarding Chauncey Billups, the Most Valuable Player of the 2004 Finals: VERY EFFECTIVE ON DRAGS, WILL BULLY TO MIDDLE, UP-&-UNDER=R SH (BASE), AVG PULLUP J, KICKS LEGS & FLOPS, BULLDOG IN POST!

In other words: SIMPLY A NIGHTMARE.

And so, as his teammates file into the locker room, Jones hustles to the court, sore foot and all, to begin preparing for his assignment. His backup, Keyon Dooling, is the fastest man on the roster, but he has special instructions to shadow Rip Hamilton, whose "quick C&S (catch and shoot)" and maddening fakes are destined to create match-up problems for Dwyane Wade.

"I already knew that," Dooling says, folding the blue scouting report in half and tossing it aside like a bubble gum wrapper. "We just have to go out there and play. I'm aware of what he can do and I'm ready for it. This is what you live for."

He's right. Scouting reports aren't worth a lick if you can't put the ball in the hole.

The Pistons smell blood from the start. With Shaq's ailing thighs limiting him to five-minute shifts, they circle Wade like hungry sharks. Jones is in no position to help—Billups has him covered at every turn. Fortunately for the Heat, Billups and Hamilton are struggling on offense, too. Detroit leads by one at the half.

With Jones in a funk and Wade searching high and low for his touch, the bulk of Miami's scut work falls to Dooling in the second half. During an official's timeout in the third quarter, the Heat guard explodes at Hamilton, smacktalking him nose to nose on the way to the bench. The two slap, grab, push, pull and cuss one another on virtually every screen play. With each handful of jersey, each elbow to the back, the venom rises. Though accustomed to such hands-on attention, Hamilton is irked by Dooling's hounding, the steady collision of skinny arms and legs. He finishes with 16 points. But Jones' man Billups steps up big, scoring eight of his 18 points in the final five minutes for a 90–81 Pistons win.

In the locker room afterwards, Dooling isn't ready to call it quits.

"You know, I wouldn't consider him a physical player," he says of Hamilton. "He does a lot of running around out there, but I don't sweat what he does."

"What was all that back and forth business between you guys?" I ask.

"I don't know, but he better know I ain't no motherfuckin' punk. He better try that shit on somebody else, because I ain't gonna back down from his ass."

Down 1–0 at home, the Heat need to find a way to counter Detroit's punishing backcourt and Dooling looks more and more like the solution. He's reed thin, but unlike Jones, he can match any guard his height in strength and intensity. No one openly criticizes Jones' effort, but it's clear that he's Miami's weak link.

Dressed again in his civilian clothes, Dooling stands up in his polished loafers and adjusts his collar. Across the room, Damon's locker is vacant. He has come and gone.

"We've got to be ready for Chauncey," Dooling says. "He's a bulldog down there."

Bulldog, eh? Sounds like he read the scouting report after all.

MIAMI, MAY 24

RICHARD HAMILTON AND THE Coatesville boys stroll into Teasers, a trendy open-air lounge on Miami's Ocean Drive, with Laron Profit of the Wizards to watch the Spurs and the Suns in Game Two of the Western Conference finals. Spreading themselves on the white leather couches, they peruse the menus as a hip-hop mix streams from the speakers. A busty, blonde waitress, whose ass cheeks hang a good two inches below the hem of her white miniskirt, takes Hamilton's order: buffalo wings, chicken fajitas, and a heaping side of French fries. She returns with the food fifteen minutes later, bending low to serve up a show. Pity I don't have any dollar bills. Between bites, Hamilton glances at the flat-screen TV in front of him, occasionally taking a sip from a virgin strawberry daiquiri. Since he's not drinking alcohol, the boys aren't either. Jontue Long, Josh Nochimson and, Profit, a former teammate from Hamilton's days in Washington, all clutch bottles of water.

Late in the game, the Spurs' Robert Horry drains one of his clutch threes. Hamilton stretches out, propping himself on the couch with his right elbow. "Man, that dude is cold," he says, shaking his head.

He tugs on his ever-present black do-rag and adjusts his Gucci shades. I try to make sense of the scene as best I can, given the intoxicating effect of my very own daiquiri—everything included. It's hard to picture these guys against the gritty backdrop of C-Ville. The soot that creeps from the brooding steel mills is no match for the warm sea breeze that dances off the ocean fifty yards away, racing inland across the sand to ruffle the skirt of the lovely waitress.

Come midnight, Hamilton will be gone, halfway down Biscayne Bay to the Ritz Carlton, where the Pistons are holed up on the eve of Game Two.

MIAMI, MAY 25

SIX MONTHS AGO, IT was unthinkable to mention Dwyane Wade in the same breath with LeBron James and Carmelo Anthony—the top two Rookie of the Year candidates from his draft class. Not anymore. In Wade, Miami has discovered a rare combination of speed, athleticism, grace, humility, skill, and intelligence—a bundle of virtues not found in any player since, well...I'm not even going to mention his name. It's too clichéd. Let's just say he used to play ball in Wade's home town.

Behind a breathtaking line of 40 points, eight rebounds and six assists from the NBA's brightest new star, the Heat strike back in Game Two to even the series at one apiece. "He got a lot of easy baskets," says Larry Brown. "But he was just phenomenal in every way."

On the last play of the game, Wade snares a long rebound off a missed jumper by Tayshaun Prince and races toward the Pistons' basket from midcourt. Miami's jubilant fans rise to their feet. At the foul line, Wade slows just a touch to adjust his steps, then explodes from the dotted half circle, extending the ball high above his head. As he elevates, he spread his legs in a manner eerily similar to that of a certain someone and thunders the ball through the hoop.

Caron Butler, a close friend and former teammate of Wade's, is sitting two rows behind the basket. He throws his hands in the air and screams just like everyone else. Wade meets his eye, nodding his head. He is standing at the baseline, his vision locked on the screaming crowd, when his teammates rush the court and swarm him.

DETROIT, MAY 27

PISTONS PR MAN KEVIN Grigg has advised the media to be at Detroit's practice facility for player interviews by 11:15 a.m. With Larry Brown running the show, that means more like 11:45. Brown's practices tend to run long. By noon, nearly fifty reporters are clogging the hallway that leads to the gym. At 12:15, I try to catch a quick catnap on the floor while two cameramen engage in a heated debate over which is the better place to watch a game, Comerica Park or Ford Field. I'm left wondering how either fool survives in the real world.

At 12:30, the gym door swings open and the press starts to jostle around. I'm not looking forward to the next twenty minutes. The Pistons work on free throws after practice, so we've all got time to adjust our lenses.

Rip Hamilton isn't in the gym. He's getting treatment on his sore right calf. Chauncey Billups, Tayshaun Prince, and Rasheed Wallace gather under one of the baskets while Lindsey Hunter goes to the line to shoot two. Hunter says something to the group and his face breaks into a huge smile. His teammates crack up. He releases a shot. Drills it. On the center court, as is his custom, Ben Wallace works on his fifteen- to eighteen-foot jumpshot—the one he seldom uses in games.

On the rare occasion when he does, I always say out loud, "That's not what the Pistons need right now."

Horace Jenkins rebounds for Ronald Dupree. Behind their basket, Darko Milicic lowers himself onto a weight machine, adjusting the pins to work on his lats. Carlos Delfino sees the Serbia and Montenegro native sitting on his own and settles into a nearby machine. It always seems to pain him to see Milicic by himself. As difficult as the season has been for Delfino, he's at least in the rotation. Milicic was informed by Brown in the fall that he wasn't going to get much playing time. No wonder he's in a funk.

After a few reps, Delfino can't resist the lure of the laughter bounding from Billups' basket. He's been struggling to fit in himself and this is an opportunity too good to pass up. The laughter continues when he joins the party. Milicic moves on to another machine.

At long last, Grigg announces that Hamilton won't address the media. No matter. I'm meeting him at the Palace in ten minutes for a photo shoot—the one that will provide the pictures for my next story in the magazine.

Hamilton walks into the hospitality lounge two doors down from the locker room wearing his game uniform and flip-flops. He looks exhausted. As he struggles to turn on the charm for photographer Ture Lillegraven, the portable speakers hooked to Lillegraven's ancient iPod belch forth this annoying mix of techno music. It doesn't take a genius to see where this is going. I rush to the rescue, scrolling through the playlist to find something with a bit more energy: 50 Cent's *Get Rich or Die Tryin'*. Hamilton snaps to life, singing along to "P.I.M.P."

"I like this album much better than the new one," he says. "It's already a classic to me."

After a few close-ups, the photographer asks Hamilton to recline on a black leather couch with a basketball in his hand. Hamilton complies and soon appears ready to nod off.

"More relaxed," Lillegraven demands.

Hamilton loosens up a bit.

"More."

Hamilton sits up.

"You gonna make me look soft lying on this couch like that," he says. "I can't have that."

Moments later, he lumbers off with me giving chase. I want to ask him a few questions about Coatesville, but clearly he's not in the mood. I tell him to enjoy the next thing on his schedule—a nap.

DETROIT, JUNE 4

IN GAMES THREE AND FOUR, the Pistons and the Heat traded blows like gladiators. Dwyane Wade scored at will in the first, leading Miami to a 113–104 win with 36 points. Richard Hamilton drew Wade's number two nights later, holding the streaking star to 28 points and adding 28 of his own for a 106–96 Pistons win.

Neither Shaq nor Billups nor anyone else on the court could tip the balance. The talking heads on TV and radio combed through the matchups, releasing enough hot air to melt the polar ice caps, but no one knew what to predict. The Pistons expended so little energy to eke out their wins, it was impossible to gauge their strength.

I did some live TV for ESPNEWS, extolling the virtues of both clubs, but I couldn't honestly tell you which was going to the Finals. It was too close to call...until Game Five, when Wade got injured.

The Heat had jumped out to a 20-point, third-quarter lead when the guard strained a rib muscle on a quick crossover dribble. He was in too much pain to finish what he'd begun. The Heat held on for an 88–76 win and a 3–2 series lead, but they enter tonight's game without their catalyst. In his place, Stan Van Gundy has subbed streaky, third-year forward Rasual Butler. The Pistons smell blood once again.

Butler hits a clutch jumper early in the second quarter to give Miami a 20–19 edge, but the highlight reel stops there. Damon Jones can't find his long-range shot. Udonis Haslem, who stumped the Pistons with baseline jumpers and emphatic slams in Game Five, can't shake Rasheed Wallace or Antonio McDyess. Eddie Jones and Alonzo Mourning, the role players who stepped up big in Miami's three series wins, simply flatline.

Late in the fourth quarter, Shaq sheds three defenders to score on a layup, snaring himself a bonus free throw. Miami's bench is lost in a trance.

In the closing minutes of the 91–66 thrashing, the big fella rides the bench, practically holding back tears. Eddie Jones sits next to him with a Band-Aid covering the stitches above his right eye. Udonis Haslem looks as if he's just been cut from the squad.

You'd never know the series is tied at three games apiece.

Damon Jones walks into the press room a half hour later in a pair of jeans and a plaid shirt—sans the sunglasses and jewelry. NBA players seem to dress down after a loss. In times of struggle, they almost resemble ordinary people.

"Will you guys even look at film of this game?" I ask.

"I don't think there's a reason to watch this game," he replies. "We understand what we did wrong."

One by one, he ticks off the team's transgressions: poor rebounding, sloppy passes, sluggish defense. "If we had just controlled the tempo and cut down on the turnovers, maybe it would have been different," he says. And then...

"This game is over and we're ready for Game Seven."

MIAMI, JUNE 6

When the storm has swept by, the wicked are gone, but the righteous will stand firm forever. —Proverbs 10:25

THE BLUE SCOUTING REPORTS are history. If the Heat don't know what to expect by now, they're in trouble. It's all about *heart* and *pride* and *faith* tonight—the three words printed on the laminated green card sitting on the seat next to Alonzo Mourning's locker. The same cards can be found at the lockers of Dwyane Wade, Eddie Jones, and Rasual Butler. The team has gone Biblical. Inside the arena, the air is positively supercharged.

When the Heat march onto the court for warm-ups, Wade is nowhere in sight. *Gulp!* Hours earlier on ESPNEWS, I reported that he'd play. His teammates need him. Miami's fans need him. You can see the anxiety on their faces. *Where the hell is he?*

When the buzzer sounds, the crowd rises to its feet in a rousing ovation. Wade trots from the locker room like he's Willis Reed himself.

Game on.

Play opens at a furious clip. With Wade struggling to recuperate, Shaq has been telling everyone in sight that *he'll* carry the Heat. He works inside for a pair of dunks to give Miami an early 9–4 lead. Rip Hamilton answers, with Keyon Dooling clawing away at him by drilling his first six shots. Laboring to find his stroke, Wade hits a twenty-two-footer for his first basket seven and a half minutes into the first quarter. He can't seem to get the lift he needs. The pressure is on Jones to raise his game.

That is, until late in the first quarter when he steps on Chauncey Billups' foot, rolling his ankle. He limps to the locker room to have it re-taped, returning to play thirty-two ineffective minutes. His final line: one point and two assists. The Heat hang on, pulling points from Udonis Haslem and Eddie Jones. Detroit counters with scrap, pouncing on Miami's guards at halfcourt, diving for loose balls and fending off Shaq's determination in the paint. And then, inexplicably, up four points with six minutes to go, Miami stops feeding the big man. "I'm not out there making decisions, so you have to talk to the guy who's making the calls," he says afterwards, visibly angry with his teammates.

When the buzzer sounds, putting an end to the 88–82 loss, Miami's fans slump in their seats in disbelief. Inside the Heat locker room, the playful banter is replaced by a chorus of whispers. The wave of good feeling is gone. Losing summons change—which means the players soon will go their separate ways, never to unite again on the court.

For days, Van Gundy had blasted the media for suggesting that his team was unbeatable. Despite Shaq's power and Wade's brilliance, he insisted the Heat were vulnerable. He was right, and he couldn't be more unhappy about it. Somewhere between the bench and the press conference podium, he has lost his sportcoat. His hair is ruffled beyond repair. He can barely speak. "I don't think from a professional sense, from a basketball sense, that I've ever been more disappointed," he says with a hundred pairs of eyes fixed on him. "I think [Miami owner] Mickey Arison, Pat Riley and GM Randy

Pfund have done such an unbelievable job putting this team together. I didn't want it to end like this."

Dooling offers the lone ray of light on Miami's scorched season. When I ask him about the long road from the 2000–01 Clippers to the 2004–05 Heat, his eyes gloss over with tears. "I found the love I lost," he says, fighting to quell the quiver in his voice. "It hurt me to lose it, but I know it's back. I remember why I love this game. Why I love to play. I feel like I'm 8 years old again. This experience has given me something I never could've expected."

I promise you he isn't bullshitting. I've known Keyon since his first day of rookie orientation. Way back in September of 2000, I interviewed him during a break in the seminar about how to deal with friends and relatives who ask you for money. "You're my dark horse for Rookie of the Year," I told him. Seven months later, near the end of his trying first season, he seemed almost embarrassed that I had put so much faith in him. "I guess I didn't live up to your pick," he said sheepishly in one of those sad Clippers locker rooms.

The sadness in this locker room is altogether different.

Dooling stands to leave. We hug. I wish him a good summer—a weak pick-me-up, but it's the best I can do.

Jones emerges from the training room, ginger-stepping toward his locker, fifteen feet from the door. He's dressed in a plaid shirt that just might be made of flannel. After dropping his jewelry and sunglasses on his seat, he turns to face the media. Tape recorders come darting at him from every direction.

"Can you sum up the way you feel, Damon?"

He exhales and drops his head, shaking it slowly from side to side. "This..."

His voice is barely audible.

"This is devastating. This is just…I can't understand…"

"Is shock what you're feeling?"

"Complete shock. This team has worked eight months for a common goal and now we've failed. This pains me to come up short. There were so many things that we could have done in the late stretches of the game that we failed to do. Shaquille wanted to take the blame, but I won't let him. As his friend, I won't let him. I love him. I love this team. I have to shoulder the blame. As the point guard, it was my job to get him the ball and I didn't do it. There's no excuse."

The next question defeats him. He pauses and clears his throat, but he can't summon the words to answer it. It's strange to see him like this, stripped of his personality, the vibrant light that flooded the Heat locker room on so many nights, the gift that drew players from all walks of life into his orbit. In the NBA's eyes, he's expendable without it.

The tape recorders click off en masse. I'm startled by the violence of the moment. It's like being seated at a dinner table with a family that's disintegrating but laboring to keep up appearances. In the silence of the room, you're struck by the silverware tapping against the plates.

The reporters break their huddle, Jones picks up his things and heads for the door. I search for something to say, but once again come up short. He's thinking about the biggest loss of his career and I'm thinking about closure.

A local TV reporter cuts me off, offering a handshake and words of condolence. Jones barely acknowledges her—a clear sign for me to step back. Nothing I say is going to comfort him. I stand down and he makes his way to the exit. It's an abrupt and awkward ending to our unforgettable journey—the best season Damon Jones ever had.

THE FINALS

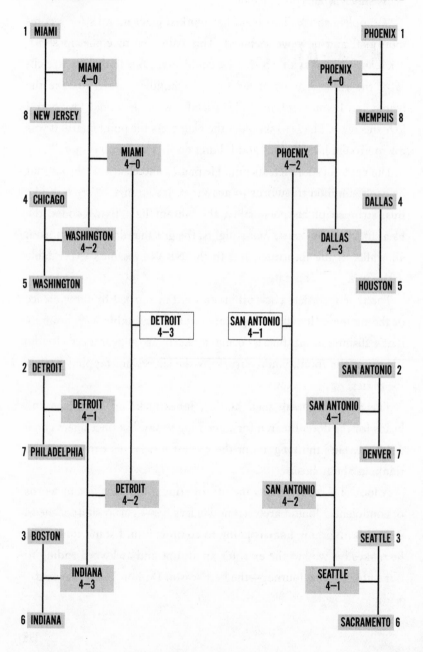

EASTERN CONFERENCE

WESTERN CONFERENCE

1 MIAMI

MIAMI
4–0

8 NEW JERSEY

MIAMI
4–0

4 CHICAGO

WASHINGTON
4–2

5 WASHINGTON

DETROIT
4–3

2 DETROIT

DETROIT
4–1

7 PHILADELPHIA

DETROIT
4–2

3 BOSTON

INDIANA
4–3

6 INDIANA

PHOENIX 1

PHOENIX
4–0

MEMPHIS 8

PHOENIX
4–2

DALLAS 4

DALLAS
4–3

HOUSTON 5

SAN ANTONIO
4–1

SAN ANTONIO 2

SAN ANTONIO
4–1

DENVER 7

SAN ANTONIO
4–2

SEATTLE 3

SEATTLE
4–1

SACRAMENTO 6

THE HEART OF A CHAMPION

SAN ANTONIO, JUNE 23

IF A SINGLE MOMENT can sum up a season, this would be it. I wish I had a camera to capture it on film. Instead I'll leave it up to the photographers lining the court, Nikons at the ready, index fingers firing away to land the cover image for next year's media guide—the snapshot that so deftly illustrates what makes this the most resilient team in sports. The Detroit Pistons starting five—Chauncey Billups, Richard Hamilton, Tayshaun Prince, Rasheed Wallace, and Ben Wallace—are huddled in the lane, arms stretched from one shoulder to the next to form a tight circle. Their heads are bowed. To a man, they have but one concern and that's what will transpire in the next two minutes and forty-six seconds.

The tallest Piston, Rasheed Wallace, drapes his left arm over the shoulder of the shortest, Billups, and his right arm over the hulking Ben Wallace. His head bobs up and down with the ferocity of his words. He screams something about Robert Horry, the marksman who decided Game Five for the Spurs with a three-pointer in overtime. Wallace's teammates nod. Watch out for Manu Ginobili, too, someone adds. He just sank a soul-crushing jumper from behind the arc and had two dunks in four minutes earlier in the night. But most of the talk is about what's at stake, the fire-and-brimstone sermon the

Pistons have heard a thousand times before—usually from Rasheed. What makes this speech different is the monumental import of the moment. There in the lane at the SBC Center in San Antonio, all Rasheed's teammates have to do is look up at the scoreboard to see that they're trailing the Spurs by seven points, 72–65, in Game Seven of the NBA Finals. Billups peeks over his right shoulder. The Spurs have left the sideline. They're walking toward him five across in that *Right Stuff* kind of way.

The Pistons break the huddle. What follows will determine how their names are etched into the history books…

I ARRIVED AT THE SBC Center in San Antonio about two hours before tip-off. The arena is cavernous, but Spurs fans have no trouble filling it with hysteria for their beloved basketball team. In San Antonio, the game has a distinctly Latin flavor. Throngs of Mexican Americans populate the upper bowl, wearing Duncan, Parker, and Robinson jerseys. When forward Bruce Bowen pulls down an offensive rebound to put a fresh twenty-four seconds on the shot clock or the firey Ginobili flops on the floor to draw a foul, they roar their approval.

I survey the scene from the padded scorers table. As the referees stretch their hamstrings and the radio guys review their notes, I just sit there taking it all in. It's as if the shot clock is winding down. Everyone's busy doing something. Everyone but me. I'm waiting for Rachel Nichols to finish her report for ESPNEWS so I can throw in my two cents on tonight's matchup.

The on-site producer gives her the all-clear signal and Nichols sets her microphone on the purse at her feet. I take a deep breath and step in front of the camera, half wondering if someone's going to bring me a fresh mic. I'd hate to use Nichols' personal microphone without her blessing. Imagine walking into the Yankees clubhouse before batting practice and snatching up Derek Jeter's bat. *Who do I consult for the proper protocol?* I don't know. And yet, oddly, I feel calm. In an instant, I'll be standing in front of millions of people talking basketball, which, as you know, is one of my favorite topics. As long as someone's listening, I'll talk hoops in a life raft floating on a river of lava. I swipe the microphone from Nichols' purse.

"Sixty seconds," says the producer.

I raise the mic to my mouth.

"Don't cover your face."

Finally, some direction.

The ESPN logo is visible on three sides of the microphone. Producers hate it when one of those ESPNs isn't facing the camera. Mine rushes me and, without saying a word, turns the mic so that the company brand invades the nation's TV screens. We're live. I boldly predict that the Pistons are going to win. They can't be denied. "If they keep an eye on Robert Horry, they'll be fine," I say.

"Thanks," says the producer, turning his attention to the feed in his ear.

I set the mic back on Nichols' purse.

I have this little tradition, some might call it a superstition. I have to walk across the court at least once during the NBA Finals. I'm usually content to go sideline to sideline, but after my brief cameo, I'm feeling adventurous. I walk diagonally.

When I played hoops in high school, crowd noise never bothered me. Inside my head, the volume was muted, even at the most critical junctures in a game. As I walk across the floor in San Antonio, I find myself once again in that altered state of mind. The sound waves disappear and the significance of the setting tickles my brain. *Who needs drugs when you can step on a basketball court?*

I remember feeling lightheaded when I took my first step onto the floor at Madison Square Garden, the scene of so many pivotal moments in the game's history. I walked from one hash mark to the other to make sure that what I saw was real. Knicks coach Jeff Van Gundy was sonorously briefing his ball club on the finer points of defending Tim Duncan and David Robinson of the 1998–99 Spurs. New York was down 3–1 in the Finals, so I understood his sense of urgency. Just the same, I was young and restless. I couldn't sit still. I scooped an official NBA ball off the rack and started dribbling. The pebble grain felt good to the touch. I closed my eyes and tried to read the Braille. This is what it must have felt like for Ray Charles to sit behind a keyboard for the first time. I opened my eyes to find the words NEW YORK KNICKS printed on the side of the ball.

My colleagues on press row were concerned with what was causing the delay. I was thinking of bigger things. I had to take a shot. I drifted toward the lane and stopped a few feet from the basket where John Starks had dunked left-handed on Michael Jordan in 1993. I looked around. No one was watching. I raised the ball and released a seven-foot set shot that kissed sweetly off the glass. *WHOA.* I ran down the ball and backed it out for a ten-foot jumper in the lane. Missed. But who cares? I was shooting hoops at the Garden. I shed my backpack and worked up a sweat, circling the basket, hoisting up shots. And then, I heard a second dribbler approach. I turned to find *SportsCenter* anchor Stuart Scott, pea green, four-button suit and all, moving in my direction. "I told myself I want to be able to dunk at least once a year," he said. "And I haven't dunked this year." He took off his jacket and started tossing up shots. One reporter after another followed. In no time, sleeves rolled up, ties flailing, the press had abandoned its post to chase down wayward balls and scream, "Hey, I made that! Kick it back out!" I'd returned to the schoolyard at P.S. 182. There were so many balls ricocheting off each other, it was easy to hide the fact that most had little chance of finding the hoop.

Before we could truly embarrass ourselves, Larry Johnson and Patrick Ewing walked out of the tunnel.

"What the...?" said a perplexed Johnson.

In a flash, the hardwood wannabes scrambled to assume their positions. I missed my last quick J and ran down a loose ball. I was now faced with a difficult decision. As any gym rat will tell you, you never leave on a miss. But how could I keep playing with everyone else crowding L.J. and Ewing to ask about Game Five. I'd look like an idiot.

Without wasting a moment, I turned and fired an eighteen-footer from the baseline, the very spot where hours later Avery Johnson would launch that jumper that clinched the Spurs' first championship. The shot ripped the cords—I'm talking so much cotton I should be hawking Hanes. I trotted to the sideline and flipped on my tape recorder.

Never, under any circumstances, leave on a miss.

Never.

The day after Manu Ginobili poured in 27 points to put the Spurs up two games to none in their quest for a third title, I was in the security line at San Antonio International Airport, preparing to board a flight to Detroit and thinking about amusement parks. The way you snake back and forth for fifty yards and get only ten feet closer to the ride. I wished the dude shouting into the cell phone in front of me had failed to meet the height requirement.

With my Harold Miner-like peripheral vision, I spotted the lanky figure to my left: Bill Russell. As in *the* Bill Russell. The greatest champion the world has ever known. Michael Jordan and Joe Montana combined can't top his ring collection.

I put my laptop in a gray plastic bin and snuck a peak at the legend bending down to remove his brown Rockports, secretly relieved to see that his NBA crew socks didn't have holes in the toes like mine. When you're a winner like Russell, you don't have to take off your No. 6 Celtics cap. The security guards are too busy sucking up to notice it.

After detouring to grab my 6 a.m. Coke (medium with no ice), I hustled to Gate 6 to find Russell sitting alone in the left seat of a three-chair row. I took the one on the right. The middle one might as well have been the Berlin Wall. Thanks to a documentary I saw on ESPN Classic, I know that Russell doesn't like to talk to strangers in public. Not even to punk kid sportswriters who know how important it is to keep the basketball inbounds after blocking a shot.

I threw on my headphones, cued up my iPod and scanned the sports section in the *San Antonio Express-News*. Russell pulled out *USA Today*. The green section. Money.

His cell phone started ringing.

I leaned into the neutral zone to hear what sage-like wisdom might stream from his mouth.

"Yeah, they really got their asses kicked last night," he said. "Have I been working out? Man, I haven't worn shorts since the Seventies."

I let out a chuckle, trying hard to disguise it as a cough.

Soon other people noticed my neighbor, the guy with the scruffy, graying beard from those Coors and Invesco commercials. A few even approached him. "Mr. Russell can you take a picture with my daughter? Can I please trouble you for an autograph? I saw you at the game last night." *No. Denied. Grunt.* I imagined him in uniform beneath the basket, eyes fixed on the newspaper, swatting away autograph seekers with his left hand. A guy in his late twenties stepped forward wearing a Boston Red Sox hat. He tapped Russell on the shoulder.

"Hi Bill, I love those great Celtic teams of the Sixties. It's really great to meet you. Can I have your autograph?"

Five seconds of excruciating silence followed, then Russell mumbled, "I don't sign autographs." The Red Sox guy looked crushed. He put on a pair of black sunglasses, returned to his seat, and quietly waited for the airline to call rows fifteen to twenty. I thought of the scene in *Jerry Maguire* where Tom Cruise asks Renée Zellweger to marry him and tears stream down her cheeks from behind her tinted lenses. So much for keeping the ball inbounds. That one was in the fifth row.

The moral of the story: It takes a big heart of steel to be a champion.

THE SPURS AND THE Pistons split the first four games in the Finals, winning two each on their home courts. They fought like warriors in Games Five and Six, winning one each on the road. With two minutes and fifty-four seconds to go in Game Seven, the Spurs ahead 69–65, Manu Ginobili moved to break the stalemate, taking a pass from Tim Duncan, loosing one hard staccato dribble, and firing that three that puts the Spurs up 72–65. The shot wasn't as momentous as the John Paxson three that lifted the Bulls in Game Six of the 1993 Finals, but it was enough to stagger the Pistons.

Larry Brown called time out. The decibel level inside the SBC Center now borders on unsafe. The mayor of San Antonio may need to declare tomorrow a citywide holiday to rest his citizens' strained throats.

When the Pistons break the huddle, Rasheed Wallace's sermon is ringing in their ears. A referee points to the sideline in front of the scorer's table. Richard Hamilton shuffles into that spot to inbound the ball. The Spurs spread the floor. Chauncey Billups rushes toward Hamilton to accept the inbound pass.

For two long seasons, the Pistons have found a way to overcome every new challenge. Tonight, their options are fading. Tim Duncan is playing at the top of his game. With 2:02 left, Billups draws a foul and hits one of his free throws. With 1:20 left, he sinks a jumper to cut the lead to four. But Detroit can get no closer. Bruce Bowen blocks Billups' next shot. Ginobili pushes the margin back to seven with a layup and two free throws.

When the buzzer sounds, the celebration seems strangely formulaic. The championship hats, the streamers cascading from the ceiling and the trophy presentation by David Stern are impressive, but they don't resonate with me like they did in 2004. The Pistons were loveable underdogs. The Spurs have three titles in seven seasons. There's no magic to Duncan, a modern-day Goliath, winning on his home floor.

Before leaving the court, the Pistons trade hugs with the Spurs. They're disappointed, but not devastated—not like the loud-and-proud Heat. What does Chuck D say? *Never let a win go to your head or a loss to your heart.* That all-important balance is a Pistons' hallmark. They never let themselves get too high or too low. They seized the Grail once. Who says they can't do it again?

Inside the locker room, reporters jockey for position as the players exit the showers. Hamilton is one of the last to emerge. His eyes look tired and his cornrows are frayed. On his arms, I see jagged lines of torn flesh freshly exposed by San Antonio's defenders.

He gives the Spurs obligatory credit, offering up nothing profound, no great declaration about a triumphant return to next year's Finals. When the questions start to repeat, he shortens the answers, punctuating his quotes with sighs. "What can you do?" he says.

I detect relief hiding in his words, an end to the intense distraction of will-Larry-Brown-stay-or-will-he-go. Hamilton doesn't reach for this convenient excuse. He knows better. The Pistons poured everything they had into this game and they lost. No shame in that.

After my botched attempt at a poetic close to the season with Damon Jones, I've learned my lesson. When the last tape recorder clicks off, Rip sidesteps the horde. I let him walk by. He looks my way. I extend my hand and we shake.

"Thanks," I say.

"All right," he replies with a nod. There's a glint in his eye. His mouth curls up ever so slightly, giving me a glimpse of those pearl-white, perfectly square front teeth.

Yes sir.

I sit in the parking lot for about an hour after the game. No radio. No cell phone. No thought to the hundred pages of notes I have to review, the hour upon hour of tape I must transcribe. I simply stare at the dashboard of my rental until the jubilant honking of the car horns fades in the distance. In the back of my mind, a small perception forms—one that won't register fully for many months. *I made it. The season is over. I have survived.*

EPILOGUE

THERE ARE NO MORE white horses or pretty ladies at my door. That's the last line from the notorious drug dealer played by Johnny Depp in the movie *Blow*. It's also how I feel right now, sitting on the tattered asphalt behind Magnolia Elementary. Who knew the NBA could be so addictive? On this court where I first discovered the joy of the game, I've always found my share of life lessons. In the second grade, I took my first punch here and struggled for a day to overcome my fear of the world beyond the classroom. In seventh grade, high atop the jungle gym, I watched a brawl between two fives, noting every blow so I could give a full report on my way home. In ninth grade, I dunked on some poor fool for the first time and laughed with my friends when he kicked the ball over the chain link fence. In tenth grade, I played future ACC Tournament MVP Randolph Childress in a thousand games of one-on-one and never once won.

At the start of the 2005–06 season, I returned to my duties at *ESPN The Magazine* a year older and a whole lot wiser. The world of professional basketball continued to turn. In October, five months after Damon Jones appeared before the nation in his Yves Saint Laurent shades, David Stern unveiled a controversial new dress code, banning sunglasses, shorts, T-shirts, retro jerseys, chains, medallions, and headphones from all league functions.

The following month, Elton Brand reported to camp fifteen pounds lighter. With his new mid-range jumpshot and two off-season pick-ups—Cuttino Mobley and Sam Cassell—he pushed the Clippers to their best start in thirty years, earning his first invite to the All-Star Game and making a bid for league MVP.

Luol Deng returned to Chicago's lineup with a surgically-repaired right wrist, fighting his way back into the starting rotation on December 10. He lost a tooth to Dirk Nowitzki's elbow and still scored 25 points against Dallas. His Bulls teammates weren't nearly as resilient. Without forward Eddy Curry, who was traded to the Knicks after refusing to let the front office evaluate his heart condition with a genetic test, they finished the month five games below .500.

On December 12, to no great surprise, Stan Van Gundy stepped down as head coach of the Heat (allegedly to spend more time with his family.) Less shocking, Pat Riley appointed himself as Shaquille O'Neal's new mentor.

Damon Jones wasn't around to lift the team's spirits. He parlayed his remarkable 2004–05 season into a four-year, $16.1 million job with the Cavaliers, quickly forging a bond with LeBron James. D.J. still considers himself the best-looking man in the league.

Keyon Dooling left Miami for Orlando. In January, he and Ray Allen of Seattle engaged in a heated shoving match that spilled into KeyArena's front row seats. The league slapped Dooling with a five-game suspension. Allen got three.

Two days later, Larry Brown won his 1,000th game as an NBA coach in New York with the Knicks—his eighth pro team since 1976. Under new coach Flip Saunders, the Detroit Pistons raced out to a league-best 37–5 start. Richard Hamilton thrived in the team's free-wheeling, fast-paced offense, reaching career highs in scoring average and shooting percentage. He too was invited to play in the All-Star Game for the first time.

In January, LeBron James ended his feud with *ESPN The Magazine*, posing for the cover and talking at length with senior writer Chris Broussard about the movie *Glory Road*. On the 16th, following the wise counsel of Bill Russell, Shaq shook hands with Kobe before a Heat-Lakers game in Los Angeles. Six days later, with Phil Jackson coaching him on the Lakers sideline, Kobe scored 81 points in a come-from-behind win against Toronto. His Nike Zoom Kobe I sneaker was unveiled on February 11.

Windows are opening for everyone, it seems, but Tracy McGrady. In early November, he aggravated an old back injury in practice, missing eight games with severe muscle spasms. On January 8, against Denver, the spasms returned, sending McGrady crashing to the floor. He had to be carted off on a stretcher. The Rockets lost all thirteen games without him. As the All-Star break approached, the team faced a steep climb to reach the playoffs. The plaintiff in McGrady's dog-bite lawsuit pleads his case in June.

As for me, here's what I've learned: The reporter-player relationship is a tricky thing. You can beg. You can smile. You can badger. But you can never really pin an athlete down. Sooner or later, like fish squirming in your grasp, they all give you the slip, leaving you to wonder how much you really knew them. That doesn't mean you can't work toward a little understanding. When Larry Brown took charge of the Knicks, Jamal Crawford lost his starting job, but he gained a wealth of maturity, making the most of every minute he had on the court. I plan to call him this summer.

Right here on this cracked asphalt birthplace is where my story ends. This court was supposed to lead me to the NBA. It didn't. I took an alternate route. From South Central to Beverly Hills, baby. To hell with my window. I think I'll hang here a while longer. My jumper needs a little work. And there's no way I'm leaving on a miss.

—Chris Palmer, February 2006

ACKNOWLEDGMENTS

A FEW YEARS AGO, *ESPN The Magazine* senior editor Jon Scher helped me create a column called CPalm's NBA Life, in which I reported first-hand the off-court activities of pro basketball players. Whenever I had too many ideas or too little space, Jon would say, "Save it for the book." Thanks, Jon, for planting the seed.

So many others in the great ESPN family made contributions. I'll start with *ESPN The Magazine* editor-in-chief Gary Hoenig for having the vision to sign off on a project like this and for never ceasing to encourage me to find my voice. His enthusiasm was matched by that of John Skipper, John Papanek, and Geoff Reiss. Thanks to executive editor Neil Fine and senior NBA editor David Cummings for bearing with me as I disappeared into my own little world for an entire season. I hope you guys enjoy the fruit of your sacrifices.

Of course, none of this would be possible if not for the players who welcomed me into their lives. To Elton Brand, Luol Deng, Richard Hamilton, Damon Jones, and Tracy McGrady, I'm forever indebted. I could not have filled these pages were they not so generous with their time. I'd also like to express my gratitude to their families and the dozens of other NBA players who helped me tell this story. And there's no way I can leave out the PR staffs of the Clippers, Bulls, Pistons, Heat, and Rockets. They never get the credit they truly deserve.

To the ESPN Books team, which spent many dreary days in New York so I could be off in places like Miami: Chris Raymond, Glen

Waggoner, Sandy DeShong, Jessica Dickerman, Nigel Goodman, and Ellie Seifert.

Gotta give two big shout outs to hardnosed fact-checkers Ian Gordon and Mike Ogle, who never once let me slide. (Sorry for making your job so tough, fellas.)

Can't forget my agents Marc Gerald and Brandon Stein of The Agency Group for their guidance and direction and *Mag* reporter Elena Bergeron for keeping me in stitches with that New Orleans charm.

I also want to tip my cap to Sam Eckersley at SpotCo for his outstanding cover design and Henry Lee, Christina Bliss, and Mary Sexton for the great page design.

In 1995, my father, Ransford, published a book called *Pilgrims from the Sun* about the financial stability of the West Indies. I knew nothing about the subject, but I was so impressed by the accomplishment that I bragged to my basketball friends. Dad, I hope you'll be half as pleased with my book.

Lastly, I want to thank my mother, Sally, who is the primary reason I became a writer. I'll never understand how someone with so much literary talent thought her time was better spent rebounding for someone destined to become a streak shooter.